Dr. D,

"Thank you for opening up your life for us! There are so many people who have been hurt and are never given the proper tool to resolve the hurt and heal from their pain. This work of art (your life) is the beginning step for many who are on their journey towards success! I appreciate your bravery in discussing sensitive topics in order to fulfill your dream of helping others and bringing awareness of those topics to the African American community when it's not the popular thing to do. You are already a success but I look forward to the further success of this project and the projects to come."

—RC

"After reading *Wrongfully Convicted*, it has given me a glimpse of all the hurt and pain one young man has had to endure. Some people would have given up on life after all this young man has gone through, but his story doesn't stop there. It's a story of overcoming life's most difficult situations and him being so transparent with his life so that others who are or were in his situation may be able to deal with and overcome their situations. This young man has received beauty for his ashes."

—PG

"It's with much excitement that I have watched you grow and walk into all that God has for you. I pray that your book reaches the nations and help them just as it helped me to live beyond my shame, hurt and pain and walk into my purpose.
I love you [and] am so proud of you!!"

—HAG

"I am grateful to have coached Danarius as he embarks on his next chapters. With the launch of his first book, *Wrongfully Convicted*, Danarius points out impactful key facts of his life that are relatable to many. No matter how dire the circumstance, how difficult the battle, how many devils seem to be attacking you— God wants us at rest, at peace, being mindful and aware, living without worry or stress, Philippians 4:6–7. I believe Dr. Danarius' vision is to relay all his struggles, strategies, and triumphant victory that has taken place within him. His purpose is to empower others who have gone through similar experiences. This empowerment can aid them in healing their self-inflicted shame, depression and all the baggage that is strongly attached to being molested. They can develop a strong growth mindset that allows them to know that nothing has to be permanent, perfect, or personal as they take charge and develop their new selves.

—"Mindful Self with Timothy McLean"

Wrongfully Convicted

Walking In Truth & Freedom

By Dr. Danarius M. Hemphill

Foreword by
Yulanda Tyre, PhD

Epilogue by
Honorable Donald Coleman
Pastor & District Court Judge

November Media Publishing, Chicago IL.

Copyright © 2018 Dr. Danarius M. Hemphill

All rights reserved. No part of this publication may be reproduced, distributed, or transmitted in any form or by any means, including photocopying, recording, or other electronic or mechanical methods, without the prior written permission of the publisher, except in the case of brief quotations embodied in critical reviews and certain other noncommercial uses permitted by copyright law. For permission requests, write to the publisher, addressed "Attention: Permissions Coordinator," at the email address below.

November Media Publishing info@novembermediapublishing.com

Ordering Information: Special discounts are available on quantity purchases by corporations, associations, and others. For details, contact the publisher at the email address above.

Printed in the United States of America
Produced & Published by November Media Publishing
ISBN: 978-0-9998274-7-5 (Print Copy)
Scripture references: KJV Bible, English Standard Version, New International Version, and Gods Word Versions

First Edition : April 2018
10 9 8 7 6 5 4 3 2 1

Contents

Dedication

Would you like to hear something funny? This is my second attempt at writing my dedication for this book. You might wonder, why a second dedication? Well, one morning while I was praying, I felt God stress the true meaning and importance of forgiveness to me.

So, on this date, January 5, 2017, I would like to express my complete and total forgiveness to my father and my oldest brother for the abuse, rejection, and disappointment heaped on me as a child. I will no longer place limitations on our relationships. Despite the negative past experiences, I forgive you and I love you. On this day, I extend an olive branch to you. I guess, in a traditional sense, I am acquitting you of your past offenses.

Nonetheless, I dedicate this book to every young man and woman who are learning to forgive themselves for the past hurts and disappointments they received from those who should have provided protection, guidance, and love.

To my father, to my family, to my friends, to my followers, to my mentors, I dedicate my story to you. I dedicate this to my sons and my daughters. I dedicate this to God for not giving up on me—for without Him, there is no me.

Foreword

Foreword: Wrongfully Convicted
Submitted by
Yulanda Tyre, PhD

In Genesis 50:20 NIV, we see a conversation taking place between Joseph and his brothers and Joseph said, "You intended to harm me, but God intended it for good to accomplish what is now being done, the saving of many lives." In 2 Corinthians 2:14, the apostle Paul says it this way: "Now thanks be to God who always leads us in triumph..."

I had the unique opportunity to meet Danarius and his mother during his first days in college. It was clear that they were very close. I had recently taken on a job at the university as a counselor in the University Counseling Center. While they presented to the center for a reason that did not include counseling, as the office offered many services, the relationship that evolved later through counseling has evolved and lingered between us somehow for over 20 years.

Danarius grew up with meager means, with a verbally and physically abusive father, a mother struggling to hold the family together, and a sexually abusive brother. Yet despite this, he has provided a transparent snapshot of his experience with the desire to not just share his story, but to help others in taking action and finding their voice. While this book at first glance may appear to mimic other stories of childhood sexual abuse both written and unpublished, this story rises to the top with a sweet aroma of success. Success is not only quantified by life, educational degrees, and a quality standard of living. It is qualified by the author's ability to act. In this book, Danarius uniquely provides supportive action steps, cognitive concepts, and spiritual support to his readers. He combines his hardships and struggles with trust, manhood, and sexuality and transforms them all into a compelling book that is approachable and practical for anyone wanting to understand the battle or break away from the darkness that sexual abuse can cast.

Through his writing, Danarius seems to sit with you and remind you that you are never in a place so dark that God cannot come and sit with you and scoop you up and take you to higher ground if you allow him to. He encourages you to look fear in the face and take a step. He pushes each of us to be like Joseph in the bible. To get out of the pit, to dream again and behold the future. He shares his heart with the intent of walking out the directives of God to be the light and salt, he shares himself so that others can share themselves...in light.

This story is more than just a man exploring—it is a bird's eye view on one man's story of his ability to take one step in the right direction. Like Joseph, Danarius have illustrated in this book whether he was in the pit, Potiphar's house, or in the prison or the palace, life could not throw anything on him that he couldn't manage. Danarius provides us with a clear picture that is the bigger the obstacle, the bigger the victory!

Words of Encouragement

Psalms 130:3-5
[3] If you, LORD, kept a record of sins,
  Lord, who could stand?
[4] But with you there is forgiveness,
  so that we can, with reverence, serve you.
[5] I wait for the LORD, my whole being waits,
  and in his word, I put my hope.

New International Version (NIV) Bible

In the Psalms 130:3-5, according to the psalmist, no matter how troubled the waters or how offended one may be by the actions of others, if through God's mercy and grace we are forgiven daily for our sins, we should be able to forgive those who have hurt us.

To many, practicing forgiveness after living a life with countless disappointments is not an easy task.

However difficult, when reflecting on Dr. Danarius Monroe Hemphill's (Dr. D) journey towards claiming his identity, it is imperative that the process of healing starts by forgiving the "person in the mirror," one's own self.

Once we forgive ourselves and allow God into our lives, Dr. D posits that we are ready to start the long walk towards realizing our purpose and true identities.

Having a firm foundation, sharing with others and being vulnerable enough to say that we have limitations are but a few of the points that Dr. D. suggest will propel us into increased self-awareness.

According to Dr. D, while we all face adversity, we should not allow it to impede our progress. He contends that we must take adversity head on and see it as an opportunity for change and growth. Moreover, Danarius argues that changing our language from a deficit framework to operating from an asset framed disposition is an excellent way to become a victor.

As an educator and one of Danarius' mentors, I am proud of his evolution and his bravery for sharing his work and journey with me, the youth in IMPACT and with the world. Given the transparency and sage advice that he provides, readers young and seasoned will be better positioned for finding their voices and stepping into their purposes.

Enjoy!
Dr. Truman Hudson, Jr.

Words of Encouragement

Surely, he took up our pain and bore our suffering,
yet we considered Him punished by God,
stricken by him, and afflicted.
But he was pierced for our transgressions,
he was crushed for our iniquities;
the punishment that brought us peace was on him,
and by his wounds we are healed.
- Isaiah 53:4-5

The author of *Wrongfully Convicted*, Dr. Danarius Hemphill, made a conscious decision that the torments of his past would not control his future. This is his story—an up-close and personal view into the life and journey of a young man who continues to struggle to know and believe just how special he is to God and to humanity.

Dr. Hemphill understands the difficulty of accepting exactly how much God loves you and how special you are in His eyes, especially when it seems you are always getting the short end of the stick. He has come to believe when God is equipping you with the tools needed to make a generational IMPACT, you may have to endure what seems impossible in order to grow, mature, and learn the lessons you will need to help others in the future. And that is the ultimate goal of this book—*Wrongfully Convicted*.

While each of us knows there will always be challenges to face in life, those challenges are easier to endure when we have a relationship with God and trust Him regardless of the circumstances or situations which come our way. Dr. Hemphill, on his journey, has made the decision to continue to trust God, hear God, and obey God—and in these pages, he shares his story.

First Lady Sherrayna Coleman

Words of Encouragement

Do you know Young Dr. D.? I have seen him in myself and I am confident he lives in each of us. We may be paralyzed by fear, anxiety, or depression, and like Young D., we encounter moments when we are still longing for approval.

Young D. sought approval throughout his childhood and through the torment of his adolescence. His conflicting views of life, trust, and family would eventually lead to plummeting self-esteem. Inside each of us, there is an inner child who was once wounded and is now scarred. Over the years, we chase that child into the shadows. But like Dr. D., his Young D. was always there, presenting unexpected impacts on his actions, his decisions, and ultimately his strength.

Some days Young D. still reaches out for approval, answers, and guidance. These days have become less frequent as Dr. D. has found his way—through his unwavering faith in God and his commitment to making the world less painful for all the Young D.'s to follow. Dr. D.'s message of the healing of his inner child resounds in the hearts and souls of all who have ever felt lost, lonely, or unloved.

Barbara Klocko, PhD

Preface

Court Is in Session
The Verdict

[Newscaster:]

Ladies and gentlemen, we're in front of the Detroit City
Courthouse,
where the verdict in the case of Danarius Hemphill versus
the world is about to
be read. They're getting ready...yes, I think they're getting ready
to return to the courtroom.

[Lady:]
Dr. Hemphill, how can you say you promote Christian values,
when you associate with secular individuals in both academia and
the business world?

[Newscaster:]
Here he comes! I cannot believe the controversy shrouding this
humble man.

[Man:]
Dr. Hemphill, is it not true that you're not a Christian, but a
secular professional posing as a Christian?

[Man:]
Excuse me, Dr. Hemphill, I'm from the Detroit City Missionary
Baptist Church. I've seen your social media, your videos, and your
message, and I can tell you this: you won't come and do that mess
in my church!

[Bailiff:]
Order in the court! Order in the court! Please rise. The Court of the Second Judicial Circuit, Detroit, Michigan, is now in session, the Honorable Judge presiding.

[Judge to the Jury:]
Have you reached a verdict?

[Jury Foreman:]
Yes, we have, Your Honor.

[Judge to the Jury:]
What say you?

[Jury Foreman:]
We the jury, in the case of The State of the World versus Dr. Danarius Hemphill, regarding the charges of
attempting to take the Gospel to the world,
making His message of hope meaningful,
and tearing down the walls of fear and rejection,
the jury finds Dr. Hemphill...

Scared and Alone

I am scared. I am alone. How did I get here? What is going on? What have I done? I do not belong here. Someone, please, come and help me! Can anyone hear me calling? I do not know what to do. I do not know where to go from here. It is cold. It is scary. Can anyone hear me calling?

I stare in wonder at the jury, as they begin to read the verdict. How could these charges be crimes for which I am being convicted? I am removed from the courtroom and returned to my cell. I press my face against the bars, holding tight as my hands shake with fear.

I look around and I am all alone. My heart beats faster. The tears fall down my face. Cold sweat envelops my body.

Wait! I hear someone. I look around and instantly see him—a little boy sitting in the corner, crying, shaking, scared, and alone. What has he done to end up here?

I turn again and see other people behind him. What are they doing here?

And suddenly I realize, we are all struggling, imprisoned in some way. It comes to me at once: one of the greatest gifts we can receive from our own struggles is when we learn the meaning of empathy—the simple ability to say to another struggler, "Me too! I understand."

Until you can override your insecurities and step into your destiny, you will never know the impact you can have. Keep in mind the stronghold that protects you from one enemy might imprison you to another.

The Price of Freedom: What Happens to the Wrongfully Convicted?

What happens to those individuals whose lives are turned upside down because of a wrongful conviction when they are finally exonerated? In addition to years of lost time and broken relationships with family and friends, they return to society in a world completely changed from when they were imprisoned. Some who have been released have been incarcerated for so long, cell phones, iPads, and Kindles are foreign to them. Even more distressing, family and friends have moved on, and so they walk out of prison, finally free, with little support, slim prospects, and empty pockets. Nearly forty percent of those exonerated after wrongful imprisonment receive no compensation.

Wrongful conviction and its effects, as discussed thus far, are spoken of in the legal sense of the words regarding courts, laws, judges, juries, attorneys, police officers, evidence, and the like. But in truth, wrongful convictions occur on a daily basis as we judge those around us and "convict" them of "their crimes" without knowing the entire story.

Wrongful Conviction in Life

We are all guilty at one time or another of judging others and being judged by those around us. It is a fact of life, and we cannot escape it. It exists as wrongful conviction without the legality surrounding the courts, laws, juries, attorneys, and evidence, but imprisons just as effectively—though without the brick, mortar, and steel cell walls of a prison.

Like wrongful convictions in the legal realm, these societal wrongful convictions take their toll on family and community. When these judgments take place, children are often the victims who must deal with issues created by adults. They also then become imprisoned, rather than enjoying childhood. This type of imprisonment does not leave us unharmed and often creates rifts among family and friends as well.

Of course, in many cases, the opposition we face is not because we are being attacked, falsely accused, or wrongfully convicted, but because we are advancing into a place we have never been previously. In those times, we are often waiting for God to say something—to give direction, hope, or guidance—while He is simply waiting for us to believe what He has already promised us.

In those times, God will step over all our mess and snatch us from situations we didn't even want to be snatched from! We are HIS! And whether we have put ourselves in a situation that has imprisoned us, or we are imprisoned as a result of another's actions, He is not going to let us remain there—wrongfully convicted—because our purpose is greater than our present problems.

The Fight of My Life Declaration (This Is It)

We must never forget our past, for in remembering our mistakes we can keep from repeating them. We must never stop fighting! We must never give up! Our voice is what is needed to change the world! Sometimes we live in defeat because we don't recognize our own value. We can't allow others, with their imposed "wrongful conviction" on our lives, to define us.

What Is at Stake?

When you change the way you think, you can change your life! I want to change the world; don't you? You and I, along with others like us, have the opportunity to educate, empower, and inspire others—especially those "wrongfully convicted."

In order to do so, we must first understand our record is expunged, we have been exonerated—by God Himself. So, you don't need the approval of others to feel good about yourself. We need to tell the world, "Weigh me *not* from the outside but rather from the inside." No matter what their conclusions may be, we need no one's permission or approval to accomplish our goals and dreams. We all came into the world separately, and in the same way we shall all return.

As I have, you need to believe everything God says about you and stay in His will!

So, shall my word be that goeth forth out of my mouth:
it shall not return unto me void,
but it shall accomplish that which I please,
and it shall prosper in the thing whereto I sent it.
- Isaiah 55:11

I'm praying for your success; I really want to see *everybody* win!

As a man thinks, so does he become.
- Proverbs 23:7

19

Who are you becoming today? Regardless of any "wrongful convictions" in your life, let's start now to learn how to harness our thoughts, and stop depending on people for our happiness. Never settle for **anything** or **anyone** in your life just so you have *something* or *someone*. Never settle for less than the best. Know your worth. Keep growing, because there is beauty in growth. Don't allow people to come into your life to use you. I know it is difficult at times but keep believing in yourself and God's promises to you. We are all in this together.

And remember, you never know what someone else is going through. Only you can control you. Stop being so hard on yourself; instead, start being proud of yourself. Stop waiting for others to congratulate you and start congratulating yourself.

I know life gets hard, but never give up! Let the struggle build you up, not break you down. Don't quit! Keep moving forward and let nothing hold you back.

The higher you go in life, the harder your past will try to bring you down. Don't let who you used to be make you walk away from who you are becoming.

Those people who don't know your path will always criticize your steps. They will "wrongfully convict" you. Don't let them stop your journey. Don't let them stunt your growth. You must keep moving forward.

Unlock Your POWER

Many times, you must go through the worst to become your best. Stop delaying your healing and growth by trying to find closure for those "wrongful convictions" placed on you by others. The only closure you truly need is knowing you deserve better!

Just because you have made mistakes, doesn't mean you are a mistake. You are not your past. God has exonerated you Himself. Don't let anything keep you from your change for the better as He has planned for you.

The first step to healing is not going back to the hurt. You cannot remove the pain if you stay in the situation causing it. Whatever you have seen or experienced in the past cannot compare with what you are going to become. Today, your days of having your integrity, peace, joy, dreams, and future stolen end.

Who are you depending on to make you happy, bring you joy, or make you whole? Decide to depend on God, who always exceeds your expectations. It is important to go from living "wrongfully convicted" to living unleashed and innocent.

From "Wrongfully Convicted" to "Unleashed Innocence"

My spiritual father, Apostle Donald Coleman, was recently teaching the importance of living an unleashed life. You might be wondering what an unleashed life is. Unleashed empowerment is to live beyond constraints, hindrances, and obstacles of the past and present, whether self-imposed, imposed by others, or by virtue of adverse spiritual forces. Living the unleashed life is driven by seven P-Keys for living:

- PROMISES
- POWER
- PURPOSE
- PASSION
- PROMULGATION
- PEACE
- PRAISE

There are several things we know and must recognize that hinder us from living in unleashed innocence.

I. **Constraints** - Things that impose limits or restrictions, preventing an event from occurring. (Proverbs 25:28: "Like a city whose walls are broken through is a person who lacks self-control.") When constraints exist, they impede or completely stop normal activities from occurring. The emphasis is on the powerlessness to move forward because of unrelated blockages rather than lack of ability or lack of resources. A good illustration is a water supply stopped by a blockage in the plumbing system. The water supply is there but cannot get through because of an internal clog in the plumbing. Constraints to our purpose are internal clogs acting as checks on our advancement before we even make the effort. Internal clogs can be the result of:

1. Rejection (Genesis 3:7-10)
2. Fears that have not been identified, confronted, and overcome (not the beneficial fear associated with respect and regard for impending danger, which causes us to take proper precautions). It is fear that brings on intimidation and timidity and inhibits our capacity to trust God, ourselves, and others. It is the fear that leads to victimization.
3. Anger (Proverbs 16:32; Psalms37:8)
4. Unforgiveness (Luke17:3; 2 Corinthians 2:10-11)
5. Bitterness (Ephesians 4:31; Hebrews. 12:15)

II. **Hindrance** - Anything that provides resistance, delay, or obstruction. A hindrance can be a person, object, or circumstance which makes a vision, direction, or journey more difficult: the act of making it difficult for someone to act or for something to be done.

1. Hindrances create a spirit of inquiry that refuses to give up.
2. Whenever there is a persistent hindrance, we must pursue a strategic   alternative to overcome it. (i.e. the walls of Jericho (Joshua 6:1, 20), the overthrow of Jebus (2 Samuel 5:6-10; 1 Chronicles 11:4-9), payment of taxes to Caesar, etc. (Matthew 17:24-27)).

III. **Obstacles** - Objects, circumstances, and people that block one's way or prevent or hinder progress. An obstacle is anything, material or nonmaterial, standing in the way of literal or figurative progress.

Strength doesn't have to come from lifting heavy objects, but more often, in finding your weakness, you discover your true strength. For example, being vulnerable is thought to be a weakness, particularly for men. In truth, vulnerability, a form of transparency, is a sign of true strength.

No Distractions

If you can't change your mind about me,
then change your path.
I'm in a season where I can't handle distractions.
- Sarah Jakes Roberts

It is time to be free! Even when we've forgiven everyone else, we sometimes fail to forgive the person who needs it most—the person we see in the mirror every day! Forgiving ourselves is often the hardest forgiveness of all. Maybe it is something in your past, or something you allowed but haven't been able to move past. When you hold on to resentment, guilt, and shame, the result is toxic. It then affects every NEW and WONDERFUL thing God is trying to do in OUR lives.

The cycle won't be broken until we stop condemning ourselves for things from which the Son of God has already freed us. So, let's not waste another day holding on to failures of the old us! We may have failed but we are not failures. We may have been "wrongfully convicted" by the world, but we are innocent. God says, "I will forgive your sins and remember them no more."

Have you ever had someone say they forgive you, but they continue bringing the supposed offense up? God says, "I will remember them no more," meaning He will not continue to bring your past back up. People do; God does not. God has already forgiven you. Now is the time to finally forgive yourself. You can't have a future until you forgive the old you. Say this and mean it, "I FORGIVE ME!"

Release the need to replay negative situations over and over in your mind. Don't become hostage to your past by continually reviewing and reliving mistakes. Don't be a prisoner as a result of "wrongful convictions." There is no need to punish and poison your future for the flaws and failures God has already forgiven. Don't keep reminding yourself of what you could have, should have, or would have become were it not for "wrongful convictions."

Forgiving yourself is crucial. If you can't forgive yourself, you can't truly love yourself and start afresh. Forgiving yourself is simply letting go of what you are "convicting" yourself of so you can move on with God. If God has moved on, shouldn't we do the same? It is time to set our inner prisoner free. God has promised in Ephesians 3:20 the future is planned for you, but you can't have the future you until you forgive the old you!

Insecurity is a lack of confidence in yourself or anxiety about yourself. Our insecurities often stem from our deepest fears of failing, falling short, and disappointing ourselves and others. Everyone has insecurities, but not everyone can manage them effectively. If your insecurities are running your life, it is time to take back control. It is time to stop lying about yourself, feeling you are not good enough, and believing you can never measure up. Remember, those "wrongful convictions" are just that—wrong!

We often get caught in the comparison trap—comparing our lives to what we "think" someone else's life is like. It is a constant false reminder (which has reached new heights thanks to social media) that everyone else is better than you, has accomplished more than you, is in a better relationship than you, or has smarter and more athletic kids than you. It only creates more insecurities within you, stifling your growth and potential—a result of the fear of not being able to compete with other's standards. Stop comparing! Get out of the comparison trap!

If people refuse to look at you in a new light
and they can only see you for what you were,
only see you for the mistakes you've made,
if they don't realize that you are not your mistakes,
then they have to go.
— Steve Maraboli

God created you and placed greatness inside of you. Greatness lives inside of you, because Greater is He that is in you than the one who is in the world. Stop believing the lies and start walking with the confidence and certainty God intended for you! Be secure in knowing this truth: "With God ALL things are possible!" Now let's get out there and be legendary!

My Story

Through the writing of this memoir, I came to understand rejection is often God's protection. Be grateful you didn't get everything and everyone you thought you wanted. God wants the best for you and He has you in protective custody!

Telling my story has not been easy. I hope by sharing my own experiences and destructive behavior you will be healed and changed. Share your story, share my story, and start a conversation.

From a young age, many men have been gender trained not to be weak and not to express emotions. Even as boys, we are often told to stop crying because we are "acting like a girl." We are constantly reminded that expressing the fact we've been hurt by something or someone makes us appear weak. We suppress our true feelings and emotions and then they become like toxins. We try to maintain control in different ways—verbally, emotionally, psychologically, etc. We need to realize it is okay to ask for help, cry, show our emotions, and express our feelings. And there we can find strength in God.

You know it's the strength of God when you can encourage someone while you are barely holding on yourself.

God comforts us in all our troubles,
so that we can comfort those in any trouble
with the comfort
we ourselves have received from God.
- 1 Corinthians 1:4

Remember, just because someone is smiling doesn't mean they are okay. Most people are fighting a battle you know nothing about.

Knowing this, I come against the spirit of depression, and I'm praying for anyone who is battling! Don't you even think about giving up. Everyone has those days they wish they could go to sleep and wake up when it was all over. But because Jesus lives, we can face tomorrow. It is all going to work out for our good!

Many times, we want to come to God in our strength. The Apostle Paul says he would rather boast in his weakness, not his strengths. Paul understood if you give God your weakness, God will give you His strength! God's strength is always made perfect in our weakness.

Even in moments of deepest despair, you always have the choice of your attitude and your direction. No matter where you are or the situations you are facing, you have the power inside of you to choose to turn to the next chapter of your life.

Please don't lose hope—your future starts now! Nothing just happens.

I waited patiently for the Lord;

And He inclined to me,

And heard my cry.

He also brought me up out of a horrible pit,

Out of the miry clay,

And set my feet upon a rock,

And established my steps.

 He has put a new song in my mouth—

Praise to our God;

Many will see it and fear,

And will trust in the Lord.
- Psalms 40: 1-3

Introduction – Where Do I Start?

Dreams versus the Dreamer
From the Pit to the Palace

For countless years, I have wondered why I was dealt the hand I was dealt. As a little child, I often wondered if it was all a result of the fact that I always snuck food out of the kitchen before the rest of the family could eat. I honestly don't know, but I do know I'm a fat kid at heart.

As I grew older, I questioned if the abuse was a consequence of my disobedience and wrongful actions. Was the rejection a result of my failure to pray enough? Did the disappointment come because I didn't trust God enough? I never quite understood the position I was in until I began to read the biblical story of Joseph.

Growing up in church, I had always heard the story of Joseph with his coat of many colors. I always thought I was like Joseph, because of all the colorful socks I wore. But it wasn't until recently, as an adult, that I really read Joseph's story and became one with it. Trust me, there are many parables in the Bible I connect with, but it wasn't until I allowed myself to become enveloped in his story that I could see the parallels in Joseph's life and my own.

After reading and studying the story of Joseph in Genesis 37, I came to the realization of this truth: "If God's favor is upon you...it is on you whether times are good or bad!" With the help of Joseph's story, I now know this to be true. Since then, I've often considered myself a modern-day Joseph! Like Joseph, I am the youngest child in my family. We both dealt with rejection from our brothers, though we desperately longed to be accepted and loved by our siblings. We both wanted to please our parents, never considering for a moment doing these things would cause tension with our siblings.

I never dreamed I would not have that brotherly connection and the love which accompanied it. I never imagined how badly I wanted to be included, or how I ultimately would face total exclusion. The more I desired to follow my brothers in their footsteps, the more they rejected me. Some would argue it was because I was the youngest—making it common to be made fun of and mocked. Being the youngest, I was taking the former positions of my elder siblings as the "crown jewel," "the conclusion," "the icing on the cake," "the last one," the "we are not having any more kids" kid. I was my mother and father's baby. I was the child who wasn't planned but was destined to be.

On this journey, I've had to battle my own inner demons regarding how I saw myself, how I felt about myself, and how I faced the pit in which I had placed myself. I did not know how to properly process the turmoil I faced as a child and a young man. A portion of me felt as if I was playing chess and life said, *Checkmate, it's your move*. At times, I felt there was something special about me, yet I was unable to place my finger on it until I began to see the relationship between Joseph and myself.

Joseph's story is amazing! He had favor on his life (from his father and God), even in the midst of controversy. I've learned along the way, everyone wants the favor of God, but everyone is not granted God's favor. Favor is such a catchy word utilized in this day and age. Favor, defined by Merriam-Webster, is "approving consideration or attention," but in the Bible, it means much more. Biblically speaking, the recipient of God's favor gains approval and acceptance along with special blessings, like grace and mercy.

Joseph's father gave him a beautiful coat, and as a result, his own family cast him aside, tossing him into a pit and selling him into slavery. Everyone, it seems, wants the favor of God. On many occasions, I hear people say, "Oh, I want the favor of God." Sometimes, people fail to realize and to understand there are challenges which come with being favored. For God to show favor on your life, often opposition arises, which ultimately highlights the favor of God on your life.

The story of Joseph illustrates that whenever you are greatly loved, there are people who will greatly despise you. Many times, we are not prepared for that manifestation of favor. Whenever favor is showcased in your life, it illustrates the magnitude of God's love for you. Favor is a beautiful thing, and we tend to think of the excitement, the joy, the pleasures, and the positivity of it. Don't get me wrong; I'm with you—one hundred percent. I think it is awesome. When God raises you up and blesses you, makes ways for you, opens doors for you, and life becomes easy for you, you are favored. While you are favored, others must work hard, and there will be people who are not going to agree with God's methods—specifically His blessings on you. This can result in people not understanding you, not liking you, and subsequently being jealous and envious of you. If you have a pure and a generous heart, this can be painful for you. I've learned that sometimes, people (family and friends) don't understand the favor of God on your life. It is what happened with Joseph. Joseph was a young man whom God not only visited with dreams, but also the ability to interpret the messages of those dreams.

God showed Joseph, through a dream, his brothers would eventually bow down before him. As a child, he went in and shared his dreams with his brothers, thinking they would be excited. I can see where the confusion could come from when out of the blue, your little brother, still wet behind the ears, with no sense of direction, and downright spoiled, comes in and says, "Hey, I had a dream. God showed me that one day, you all would bow down before me." I guess that could cause some confusion. I get it, but to throw your brother into a pit to die? That was a little, no, very extreme. Even though his brothers threw him inside a pit, their action did not remove the favor of God from of his life. It didn't hinder Joseph from achieving his greatness—greatness God intended. It was the catalyst which launched, compelled, and pushed him into his destiny, resulting in Joseph becoming the second in command to the pharaoh, aka the prince of Egypt.

Have you ever shared your dream or a vision with someone? A dream you knew God had given you, only to find they weren't excited and/or happy for you? This is exactly what Joseph faced. He put his dream on the table for all to see, and his brothers joined forces against him, deciding to kill not only the dream but also the dreamer.

As Joseph shared his dream, I can imagine his brothers' hatred and envy festered inside of them. It was the icing on the cake. His brothers knew he was their father's favorite child, and they couldn't understand why he had so much favor in his life. So, they plotted to get rid of him, because when you are truly blessed, many people won't even look at you—they don't want you around, they don't want to share the same air and space with you. In this case, the brothers didn't want to share their father, and so Joseph's brothers got rid of him.

It is one thing to fall into a pit. It is another still to crawl into the pit on your own. But, it is truly a tragedy when those you love throw you in the pit and leave you for dead. That is exactly what Joseph's brothers did.

Favor is not determined by your circumstances, regardless of your disappointment, rejection, shortcomings, and most importantly, your pitfalls. Favor is still in your life irrespective of your geographic location. What we can say is God is both completely wise and supremely sovereign. He tailors His wisdom to the journey of our individual lives and uses His sovereignty to show favor to whomever He wills at the time He wills it. From a human perspective, favor often appears unfair, but when you factor in God's sovereignty, you cannot say His favor is not fair. He does what He wants when He wants, and to whom He wants.

Favor often does not seem just when it is obvious, when you see it or feel it. When it is manifest, it is simply an outward expression of inward reality. Or put another way, favor eternally exists manifesting in real time. Hopefully, you are able to see the favor of God as you begin this journey with me—as we experience real battles, real results, and real scars from having been wrongfully convicted.

Chapter 1
Make a Decision, Follow by a Single Step...

I never thought for a moment I would be granted the opportunity to write a book sharing my story on a platform of this magnitude. Now, the weird part is truly not knowing where to begin. Have you ever been there? The place of not knowing where to begin; how to make that first effort in the right direction? The place in time when you are prepared to do something great or ready to make a change, and don't know where to start or how to pinpoint your next step? Guess what? That is exactly where I am as I begin to tell my story. When you are here, the funny thing is you know the moment is upon you and the time to act is right now. And yet, you do not know what exactly you should do or where to begin.

If you have experienced it, you know this stuck place is painful, mainly because it is so very frustrating. You are ready to move forward, you are ready to do the work. You have all this potential energy, built up and bubbling over, available to make something amazing happen, something that has an incredible and positive impact. By not using it, what you create for yourself is a massive energy leak. One thing is certain: if you don't address the leak early on, it is only going to create a huge mess at the end. At this thought, you feel drained, as if all your energy has leaked away. It is as if someone attempts to give you water, but you have no vessel to carry it in. You try to use your hands and it just slips away through your fingers. It feels like your checking account is overdrawn and there is no money flowing in. I know I am not the only who has experienced an overdrawn checking account. That is exactly where I am as I begin this book. It is an awkward space to be.

Let me be the first to say, this is only the beginning. For each of us, no matter how difficult our past, this is the place where we feel awkward and unsure if this is truly where we want to go. Nevertheless, this is exactly the place to begin our journey. We need to decide to share and overcome, to take the first step into our bright and successful future, declared innocent and expressing true forgiveness to those who have wronged us. One thing is certain: either you continue to stay in this uncomfortable and awkward place, or you can make a positive, confident decision and take the first step in the right direction.

Note, I said make a decision and then take a step. Most of the time we make a decision and never make the step, and then we are stagnant, wondering why we remain in the exact position where we began—only to realize we never made the first step. We get so excited about our ideas, we totally forget we're not moving forward. We become enthusiastic about our brainstorming and decision-making and forget to perform the action and forward momentum needed to jump-start the idea or the decision.

Finally, I made my decision to begin writing and share some of my life experiences. Some are pleasant and others are painful, but each highlights the major points in my life I believe have played a vital part in my development and growth. These experiences, good and bad, shaped my ideals, my values, and my ideologies. The intent is to utilize this opportunity as an open, life-changing dialogue that will help us make the decision we need to make and take the first step forward in victory. I believe allowing others open access into my life will grant the opportunity to see lessons learned, the pitfalls overcome, the calamities conquered, and ultimately the beauty exchanged for ashes.

One day, I was talking to my friend, Hailey, while we were driving around Washington, DC, expressing my interest in writing a book.

She looked over and said, "What makes your life story any different from anyone else's? Why would someone want to read your story? What makes your story so significant?"

And in that moment, I begin to question whether I should share my story. Was my story worth sharing? What was my intention for sharing my story? These were some of the many questions swimming around in my head.

At first, I felt disappointed, because I somewhat agreed with her. I questioned, what would be my contribution? What made my story different? And instantly, I began to think about my experiences. I once heard that life is a university and classes are always in session, and I truly believe this to be true. Life is a university, and if you know someone who has attended a university, you know many people can attend the same university and have unique, completely different experiences. One may major in theater, while another student majors in business. One may have pledged a fraternity or sorority, while another was part of a different type of social organization; nevertheless, each one had distinct experiences, totally different from one another while attending the same university.

Ultimately that is what makes my story unique. I was also reminded—stories have the power to transform our perceptions of the world and ourselves. I have found the best lives are the ones filled with the finest stories. These stories give meaning to the events of our lives. It is the power of a narrative. We all articulate our stories in some way. We tell stories of how we met certain people; about the idiosyncrasies we have acquired and why; and even how the stories have helped give meaning and shaped the events of our lives. Thomas King stated, "The truth about stories is, that's all we are." It is critical for us to share our stories because it allows others the opportunity to connect. Our stories are the gateway, serving as tools for helping others find a way to escape.

Jesus often used stories set in real-life situations to aid in teaching and reaching others. They are called parables and stand today among the greatest teachings in the world. And so, I stand firm on the idea that someone is waiting for you to tell your story of how you became you, in order for them to become them.

I have always felt someone else's destiny was tied to my purpose, that we are all intertwined, woven together in a unique way. So, when I had a moment to reflect on and consider my agenda and my intent in writing this book, I wanted to share my story and allow others access into my often wonderful, though sometimes difficult, life.

Make a decision, followed by a step...

Over my lifespan of thirty years, I have learned it is imperative to have the ability to make a sound decision, as well as what it means NOT TO ALLOW THE DECISIONS OF OTHERS to define your life. Equally important is never failing to make a decision that could greatly impact your life.

In all honesty, I have been on both sides of the spectrum. Due to fear, anxiety, and uncertainty, I have allowed the decisions of others and the failure to make my own decisions to impact me greatly. You see, uncertainty is a situation consisting of imperfect and/or unknown information, and in certain stages of my life, I struggled with the idea of making my own decisions versus allowing the decisions of others to dictate my every move. But, what do you do when decisions are made without your consent, approval, and/or consideration? What do you do when life-changing decisions are made for you, and you are left with the responsibility of picking up the pieces?

Growing up as an African-American boy in the city of Detroit, Michigan, it was difficult for me to find my way. Early on, I thought my family was an ordinary family, and yet again it was not. As a little boy, my father was my "superman" and my "champion." My mother was my "wonder woman," a truly loving woman of virtue and character. I am the baby of the family, with two older brothers and an older sister, who is my pride and joy.

When I began school, things changed in our house, or maybe it was simply the time when I was old enough to understand. I lived in a household with abuse, drug addiction, and mental anguish.

Having come up in the church, thanks to my mama, I came to a point where I often found myself asking God, "...why me, why us?"

As the youngest of four children, it seemed as though the enemy took a glimpse into my future. I was born with undeveloped lungs and a heart murmur, which ultimately proved to be a stepping-stone to my future success. I was an unassuming child, who at five years old witnessed the first signs of drug addiction and physical abuse.

My father (my "champion") would enter our home after being absent for weeks and begin a simple conversation with my mother. Quickly, the situation would violently escalate. She asked simple questions, as any wife would when her husband showed up after being absent for a month or more. She questioned where he had been and his duty to our family. (I never knew what angered him more, but I'm guessing it was the latter because, in spite of it all, he was a proud man, who deep down inside wanted the best for his family.) As the conversation continued, he would become enraged and strike my mother in front of my siblings and me.

My older brother, at this point, began to try to intervene to protect my siblings and me. However, at the age of sixteen, his protection was very limited. He became so consumed with protecting us, there was no one to protect him.

At the end of the day, we still had a roof over our heads, although we may not have had our basic necessities like electricity, gas, water, and sometimes even food.

My mother struggled to make the minimum payments on the utilities and keep everything on for us, but with a meager paycheck, she could not make ends meet during my father's disappearances.

Despite my early upbringing and my relationship with my father, today I can say I don't blame him. He was never taught to love and as a result, he was too ill to learn or teach us. A wise man once said, "...smiling faces tell lies," and I can attest it is true indeed. My home looked like any other in our West Detroit neighborhood. On the outside, we were smiling and holding it together, and on the inside, we were living hell on earth. And, at the tender age of five, there are certain things a child shouldn't have to experience.

This is my story. The story of the child who still cries out inside the young man. The child who wants desperately to escape but is too afraid and finds himself unable to seek shelter within the man as a result of his fear.

Have you seen *Antwone Fisher,* a movie about a naval officer who experiences horrific hardships as a child? Fisher's words ring loudly in my mind:

"Who will cry for the little boy, lost and all alone? Who will cry for the little boy, abandoned without his own? Who will cry for the little boy? He cried himself to sleep. Who will cry for the little boy? He never had for keeps. Who will cry for the little boy? He walked the burning sand. Who will cry for the little boy? The boy inside the man. Who will cry for the little boy? Who knows well hurt and pain? Who will cry for the little boy? He died and died again. Who will cry for the little boy? A good boy he tried to be. Who will cry for the little boy, who cries inside of me?"

In listening to the echo of his words, I began to stare at my own "little boy" in the mirror. As he cried for help and inner peace, I refused to touch him. The "little boy" I am referring to is my five-year-old self.

As a kindergarten, my eldest brother, Malik, was responsible for picking me up from school. It seemed so cool at first, because, though I did not know him well due to our age difference, I still looked up to him. After we got home, he played video games with me—at first.

Then, what began as two siblings playing video games soon escalated into molestation. I was afraid and so confused. I had many questions, but no answers. After the fact, I felt as though he'd shattered so many of my dreams, dreams that I could never get back.

My innocence was stolen, taken away from me forever. I wanted to tell my parents, but even though I was only five, I didn't want to add more trouble to an already disturbed home. And so, I kept it a secret.

This secret would haunt me for years of my life. For a long time, I just wanted to lock myself in a cage and throw away the key. As an innocent seven-year-old, I didn't know if this was something brothers "did," or if it was as WRONG as it felt to me!

The molestation didn't stop there but became an ongoing process. I began to develop a mindset whereby I blocked out the physical abuse and tried to think of other things...

As an adult, even though the physical abuse stopped, I didn't know how to make it go away, how to get it out of my heart and mind, how to move on with my life. Until the day I made my decision and took my first step...

I knew I had to be my authentic self with God. It would be the only way I could keep from giving the power and influence to those negative feelings, as well as the person who tried for so long to negatively impact my purpose. The decision made...I had to make the step.

Chapter 2
Step in the Right Direction

For as long as I can remember, I have always wanted guidance and direction. I have always been open to receiving it as I navigated throughout my life's journey. I can remember growing up and wishing someone would tell me specifically how to navigate through this journey. I wanted someone to tell me the steps they had taken toward success, what roads to look out for, what roads to take, and what obstacles to avoid at all costs. Most times, throughout this journey, I felt like I was waiting for my "superman" to arrive and to save me...

My father, who held this title of "superman" for me as a tiny boy, was often absent when I most needed his guidance. Sometimes when he was with us, it seemed he would be the father and provider I longed for; other times he was frighteningly abusive. And yet, I knew he loved us, in the only way he knew how, while we feared and revered him. He truly wanted us to succeed and, I believe, would have been willing to make it happen by any means possible.

My mother, my "wonder woman," worked hard to provide for and protect my siblings and me. She provided guidance, as much as she could while hiding her own pain and fears, encouraging us to be with her—always involved in the church. She was and is a strong woman, standing through the abuse, the disappointments, the cheating, and the hardships, while always loving us and praying about the circumstances in which we lived. And yet, she could not leave, telling us to keep the secret and pray about it, nor could she be the "superman" who rescued me...

And so it was, the countless nights of me praying, as a child asking God why all this was happening to me and praying for his help; and as an adult, asking God to give me a sense of peace. For a season of my life, I felt as though God granted me my petition and led me to believe I was taking a step in the right direction.

I had to learn fulfillment in life comes from being content and satisfied. Being fulfilled requires being emptied of the trappings of this world. The trappings are those things we think are good for us, will improve us, or make us acceptable (i.e. a bigger house, newer car, a more stressful job, or new gadgets, all of which equates to more debt). We must be ready to leave it behind serenely, free of every last idea, invention, revelation, dream, insight, purpose, business, family member, or accomplishment, in order to gain fulfillment and contentment.

And even though I understood, there was still conflict inside me.

Stepping Forward and Not Looking Back

I needed to reset. I needed to not allow my negative circumstances to impact my progress forward in the right direction. It is what we all need, the ability to take the step and move forward, never allowing our past circumstances to hinder us. There were so many times, as I was attempting to step forward, when my past haunted me in an effort to keep me in fear, to prevent me from growing, to have me constantly questioning if I was making the right decision for my own life.

These are the times when it is critical to understand the seriousness of not taking the step forward. The truth is, when you change the way you think, you can change your life!

Let me encourage you, right here and now:

❖ You Have the Power within YOU!
❖ You Have What It Takes to OVERCOME!
❖ You Can Do This, One STEP at a Time!

There are days you can be really blessed and still be burdened. Days when your heart cries out, "I can't take it anymore!" I get it; I understand. I have been there...it has been the cry of my heart as well...we have all experienced it.

No matter how deep your hurt, how severe your pain, how dysfunctional your environment, you must understand—everyone has a challenge to overcome. The point is, we cannot stay where we are and accomplish our destiny; we must take the step forward. And even when fears enter our hearts and minds, we can move forward, making progress, no matter how small. The steps are not easy, and regardless of their size, they are moving you forward, in the direction you want to go.

Have You Ever Considered This About Your Current Situation?

Pressure doesn't have to break you. Instead, pressure can actually strengthen you and prepare you for greater things to come.

Never Forget: You're not alone. During lonely days or in the darkest nights, remember that God is always with you. Ready to help you, hold you, and guide you into His favor, the future He has for you. Remember too that you are not alone in your trials; others have gone before you and overcome the pressurized situations and circumstances you are facing today. And their stories, like mine, can help you overcome and move forward in victory with your life.

I had to learn in the midst of my trials and tribulations that the reality is, you are not going under . . . you're going over. You are not going to be overwhelmed . . . you're going to overcome. You are not going to come up short . . . you're going to rise above. Despite the hand of cards I was dealt, I had to learn those principles and how to apply them to my life. Regardless of how I felt about myself, what others were saying about me, and the labels that were placed upon me, I had to come to a place where I could own those powerful words.

I believe everything I went through as a result of my childhood struggles was only preparation. Merriam-Webster Online Dictionary defines preparation as: "the action or process of making something ready for use or service or of getting ready for some occasion, test, or duty; a state of being prepared: readiness." I had to learn I am better than my circumstances.

I asked myself over and over how I should begin to write this book. It is not an easy task for me, by any means, reliving the abuse, disappointments, and hardships of my childhood and the pain, suffering, and shame that lingered, for a time, with me into adulthood. No matter what you may say, writing about your life is not easy, particularly as I reopen my family's crises and experiences.

For so long, after the many testimonies I had given concerning my life and my past experiences, I thought I had finally put the past to rest. Furthermore, I didn't want to blow things out of proportion and glorify the pain of those experiences, nor cause greater pain to those involved in my memories.

Once again, I asked myself, where do I and how do I begin? That is, until I understood it was time for me to step forward and to stop looking back. I had to understand it was all only preparation for my destiny. The same is true for you: take your step forward and stop looking back. You don't have to face the same struggles and frustrations repeatedly.

As I said, there were many times I just wanted to lock myself away from my past, from everyone and everything that reminded me of what I had been through. As a young child, I had no point of reference or way of understanding the victimization I was experiencing at the hands of my brother. When it didn't stop, but became seemingly unending, I developed a mindset in which I blocked out the physical abuse by trying to think of anything that made me happy.

Needless to say, I began to become accepting of the situation, believing there was nothing I could do to make it stop. In all honesty, it didn't get any better, but soon after it became even worse. It seemed just as my brother stopped abusing me, the horror began again, anew. The only difference was this time the predator was a friend of our family. My brother's friend, a boy who was five years my senior, began paying attention to me, filling in the gaps I felt existed in my life. Part of me blocked myself out of the situation, while another part of me became compliant and comfortable. I stopped resisting, though I was afraid, believing his actions and mine were inappropriate, while at the same time appreciating the attention he was giving me. I was in a state of confusion, fearful of being exposed and equally fearful of losing the attention bestowed upon me.

And in my mind, I cried out, what was the problem? Had I become a target for abuse? Why wouldn't anyone help me? Why would no one protect me? Where was God?

This again became an ongoing process. However, this time my prayers were answered, because the perpetrator was caught by my mother. I was only eleven years old! Eleven years old, and already I had been a witness to the abuse of my mother and a victim of molestation—all before I hit puberty.

At this point, I began to ask questions of myself. Was I gay? Did being a victim of these molesters make me a homosexual? I began to shy away from all things masculine. I wasn't athletic. My voice wasn't changing like the other boys in the neighborhood who were my age. I wasn't developing either. These characteristics manifested in me being called gay, a punk, a faggot, and a few other derogatory terms.

Could everyone see my pain? Why was I being persecuted? I hadn't done anything wrong, or had I? These questions began to consume me, until I reached ninth grade. For three years, I had struggled to find answers by reading the Bible, seeking pastoral counsel and advice, all to no avail.

When my ninth-grade school semester began, I had the pleasure of meeting two high school counselors who ultimately blew my mind. It seemed as though God's grace began to show up and show OUT! These two amazing counselors helped me develop character, discipline, motivation, and gave me direction. They taught me it was not about where you have been, but it's always about where you are going. They encouraged me, telling me I was not in the fight alone. These would be the first two women I would let in, and as a result, they truly helped me.

With their support, I became active within my school's culture. I won the title of homecoming king, was elected senior officer, and became a member of the school's prestigious step team. The name-calling didn't cease. Ultimately, I am glad it didn't stop. From it, I learned true leaders did not need to demand respect; it was given to them because it was due. And although the respect was there, the demons were as well.

I began to be tormented in my dreams. I felt as though I was literally losing my mind. However, I continued to smile, place others before myself, and seek understanding in the Word. I began to encounter more encouraging people and attempted to encourage myself.

As high school graduation approached, I finally opened up to my parents. I stopped hating them, and began to seek their help. At first, I only talked a little at a time, spoon-feeding them, as it were, and all the while I was still struggling to find my own inner peace. As this newfound relationship with my parents was growing, I decided to let all my secrets escape in hopes of being free of the pressure once and for all!

At eighteen years old, just as I prepared to attend Alabama State University, I told my parents about all the hurt, abuse, and torture I had experienced. I poured out my feelings without any filter. Toward my mother, I felt disappointment and even anger. How could she remain in a marriage in which her youngest child was continually abused, with the ultimate goal of hurting her deeply? Toward my father, I felt disappointment and believed him a failure as a father. How could he abuse me, "his baby," and allow me to be molested by his firstborn, my oldest brother, but also a family friend? Where was he as my protector? I also felt anger at him, believing he could have molded my identity and helped me avoid much of the sexual confusion I was facing. I am often asked myself what sons need from their fathers. My answer really boils down to a few simple but critical things that every good dad must do, built on a framework of providing, nurturing and guiding. Nevertheless, for a moment in time, it seemed like our relationship was finally getting better and that the father and son relationship I always dreamed of was becoming reality.

We begin to cultivate a more conducive relationship where we begin to communicate more, laugh at each other and begin to gain a better understanding of each other. I no longer had to worry and or concern myself with the thoughts of, if I matter to my dad or not? If my dad loved me or not? And whether or not my dad was proud of me? I learned the primary way that dads can help their boys understand that they matter is by making them a priority over the myriad demands that life throws at them and I began to see that.

Even so, it seemed as though life was finally beginning to look up for me. And it lasted for a short while, until my father passed away on November 21, 2004. I was away at college when I got the news. Sometimes, I believe he died of a broken heart.

The Bible says, "...God is not Man, He cannot lie and His Word shall never return unto Him void..." This scripture chronicles my life. God made me a promise and it wasn't until now, stepping forward to write this book, that I was able to walk into my season. A season of overflowing and prosperity. A season where I could finally realize and accept my gifts.

All the things I have been through were only preparation for reaching my destiny. It has all shown me if I am to minister, preach, and prophesy, I must first understand where my people are in life, what they are experiencing, and try to walk in their shoes.

I often ask myself, "Why am I having so many sleepless nights?"

And I hear God respond, "Weeping may endure for a night, but JOY comes in the morning." Joy is putting JESUS first, others second, and yourself last.

So, the question remains, "Where am I now?" I am still seeking God, I am still within my season, and I am still a man of courage and faith.

The same can be said for you. Your negative circumstances can, like mine, be preparation for your destiny. You only have to make the decision and take the step forward. Don't allow fear of your past to keep you from growing and moving forward.

Chapter 3
In the Case of a Stolen Identity (War between Two Worlds)

A Case of Stolen Identity

Identity (ID) theft is a crime in which the thief steals your personal information—full name, social security number, address, phone numbers, date of birth, and so on—to commit fraud, applying for credit, filing tax returns, and getting medical services. These acts then damage your credit status and cost you valuable time and money as you attempt to restore your good name. You may not realize you are the victim of identity theft until you experience the consequences in the form of mysterious bills, credit collection calls, or denied loans coming as a result of the thief's actions.

The important things to remember if you become a victim of identity theft are:

- **Report it immediately, and**
- **Work to protect yourself and respond appropriately if it happens.**

Identity theft is a crime, plain and simple. It is the deliberate use and abuse of someone else's identity.

Identity Lost

Now you may be wondering, what does identity theft have to do with what is being discussed here? Let me explain: Due to the fact that I was molested, I struggle with my personal identity and sexuality. The realization that I was in trouble, struggling to the point of being consumed by the molestation and abuse, created in me a need to know why my father and my brother would behave in such a way. I became so focused on the views and opinions of others that I began to embody everyone else's expectations and ideas, totally forgetting who I was in the process.

My father played multiple roles throughout my life, sometimes my champion, at other times my abuser. I grew up afraid, never knowing, if my father came home from work, who he would be: my father my hero, or my father my abuser. Most often, the bad days outweighed the good.

It seemed as though the abuse came out of nowhere, erupting into nights filled with screams and violence. The abuse was all too real, but I understood the reasons behind it. It often began with a verbal attack on my mother, followed by subsequent attacks on my siblings and me. I was often his primary target—as the youngest, it seemed the abuse aimed at me was intended to inflict greater pain on my dear mother.

As a result, I grew up fearful, scared to say anything, afraid to look the wrong way, and frightened of doing anything that was considered outside of normal. I sought a safe zone in my mind, which often manifested itself as a cell, into which I could run, shutting the door behind me for protection from the abuse, hardships, and disappointments.

Then came the molestation at the hands of my eldest brother, and no one there to speak on my behalf or protect me. My abusers were two men who could have influenced me greatly and been my champions, but instead, my identity was lost amid abuse which no child should ever experience.

I can now say the damage was great, but I was not destroyed. In the Bible, the story of Joseph is told in great detail. One thing I admire about Joseph was he never allowed disappointments (and he had many) to define his life. Instead, Joseph determined early on that his life would be defined by the presence and promise of God. Whether he was being mistreated by his brothers, including being sold into slavery, facing false accusations from his master's wife, serving as a dream interpreter for the king, imprisoned falsely, or ruling over Egypt, Joseph knew who he was, whose he was, and who was always with him.

Given the difficult circumstances he faced through no fault of his own, Joseph had every right to play the victim. Instead, he chose to allow the hand of God—not his hardships—to write his headlines. And finally, as the second most powerful ruler in the land of Egypt, he was able to look back at his life and say to the brothers who sold him into slavery, "You intended to harm me, but God intended it for good to accomplish what is now being done, the saving of many lives." (Genesis 50:20)

I couldn't see it then, in my early life, when I lived in fear of those who should have been my protectors, but God's hand was at work in my life and continues to be today. You may not be able to see it at this moment in your life either, but God's hand is at work. And if you will choose to trust Him, that same hand can write your headlines, just as He did for Joseph, just as He is doing for me, and a multitude of others.

A War between Two Worlds (Help Me)

Eventually, my eldest brother was imprisoned for fifteen years. Countless times, people have told me I did not know what it felt like to be imprisoned. Sure, I'd seen prisons depicted in films and television shows like *Oz, New Jack City, The Wire*, etc., so I had a good idea of what prison was like. But contrary to the notion that I had no idea what it felt like to be imprisoned, in truth, I was in prison, in my mind. Yes, the same "safe" prison I had created as a child remained with me in adulthood, though I appeared to be walking around freely.

Incarceration is the state of being confined in prison, or imprisonment. It is associated with the synonyms captivity, immurement, and imprisonment. The state of imprisonment is always difficult and creates dysfunctional habits of thinking and acting out during periods of post-prison adjustment. The effects of being incarcerated vary from person to person; not everyone who is incarcerated is disabled or psychologically harmed by their imprisonment, though few people are completely unscathed by the experience. At the very least, prison is painful, and incarcerated individuals often suffer long-term consequences from having been subjected to pain, deprivation, and extremely atypical patterns of living and interacting with others.

Currently the United States incarcerates more of its citizens than any other country. With approximately five percent of the world's population, the United States houses twenty-five percent of the world's prisoners (Parent 1999, Stern 2005). Michigan's incarceration rate is below the national rate, at 628 inmates per 100,000, while the city of Detroit has a crime rate higher than 48 states.

Incarceration exists because it is said to lower crime, and yet something is missing from the statistics. With all the data being shared, the one thing not being reported is the number of individuals currently walking around the world physically free, but completely incarcerated within their minds.

The use of long-term incarceration as a method of legal punishment is a modern idea, originating in the late 18th century.

The same Lord who brings inner freedom also desires to see prisoners set free from their physical imprisonment. Incarceration applies to a person confined in a facility intended to restrain the person's movement and freedom, and includes prisons and other penal institutions like hospitals or other treatment facilities serving those who would otherwise be confined in prison, but for the condition being treated by the hospital or facility. In addition to those confined thusly, incarceration also includes confinement in personal living quarters with the use of electronic monitoring.

The Incarceration of the Mind

Often not considered are those who are imprisoned by their past experiences or life's ongoing circumstances. For many years, suffering under the abuse of my father, I was imprisoned by my fear. Without an adult to champion me, I lived in complete fear. Later, when the molestation by my brother began, I lived in both fear and uncertainty. What if someone found out? Did I do something to deserve this treatment? Did being a victim of molestation make me a homosexual?

Conflicts, uncertainty, disappointment, and fear molded my being and sent me flying into my own self-inflicted prison in my mind—the only place where I could find the safety I craved. Everything in my life was uncertain; I never knew what would happen next. Would my father explode violently into our home after disappearing for weeks? Would my brother pick me up from school and the molestation begin anew?

One truth in life is sure: people prefer certainty. As a child, I observed the fathers of my peers and desired the certainty and surety they had in their fathers. I saw fathers who were active in their lives, protecting them, adding value to their lives, molding their identities, and giving them purpose.

I wanted that, but my dad was not there, and so I struggled, with fear, sexuality, and low self-esteem. Even still, today, I struggle with the idea of homosexuality. I struggle with the idea of change, and yet I know change is the only certainty in this world and its pace is ever increasing.

Here is where my story of carving out a "sustainable pathway" to help others struggling with homosexuality and change can be quantified and thus shared. I have learned this process can only occur when the journey is aligned with an unrelenting commitment to spirituality, honesty, hope, and new horizons. It means navigating steep learning curves. My passion, indeed my burden, is to ameliorate the suffering of others by providing open corridors of both enlightenment and empowerment which serve as bookends for staying the course. My bouts of discouragement notwithstanding, the cost of quitting and giving up is far too great. And so, I share with you my journey.

One thing I had to learn is that I live in my head and know where the logical dots are. My journey is multidimensional and involves bringing a sense of answers and closure to the physical and spiritual dimensions of my experience, while challenging myself to accept the truth about who I am foundationally and spiritually. Looking at the spiritual dimension of who I am will give me the wisdom to plot a pathway forward based on strength, fortitude, and unyielding confidence. I am increasingly convinced that our primary answers, the ones which really matter, are sourced from internal positions rather than reactions to our external environment. Take, for instance, the revelation I got only a millisecond ago.... I came to realize when ACCEPTING my experience with homosexuality, that accepting just means I don't have to be ashamed of the route God has taken me to deliver His people. Accepting does not always mean I accept the WHAT of an experience, but it can mean I realize that only with God can I accept the WHY.

A major part behind the purpose of this book is to help others who are experiencing like struggles and are seeking spiritual/Biblical understanding. I believe everyone needs to know what the Word says specifically concerning this issue (homosexuality) and how I am dealing with my "journey" as a person who is saved by God and totally dependent on my relationship with Him.

You cannot ignore what you need to talk about. My vision for this book is to give voices to many young men and women and bring understanding and healing to them as well as to myself. Whatever struggles you are facing, it is my vision that this book will share with the you, the reader, the guidance and support needed— which I did not get.

Give what you didn't get.
- Bishop T.D. Jakes

There is a law called reciprocity, and God has an amazing way of subsidizing what you didn't get. Seek out a spiritual father or mother if your biological parents fell short of expectations. Spiritual parents make deposits in you from which you can make withdrawals for the rest of your life. They can build a special foundation with you, so you know you're not alone.

I certainly cannot reclaim yesterday, but I can embrace and celebrate today. Your story begins before you even arrive. My question of my family and friends has always been, "If you really see my failures, will you still love me?"

I have learned that even when I can see the worst in those around me, I can still believe the best for them. It is a void everyone needs filled in their lives.

Remember, you can't take a picture in the dark—you must have light! I don't always have to be a part of the picture, especially when God has called me to be the light for the picture. God has also called you to be light to others in your lives, those whom He seats at your table.

Do you know who is at your table? And the reward for ministering to those whom God seats there? He tells us clearly in His Word.

> You prepare a table before me
> in the presence of my enemies:
> you anoint my head with oil;
> my cup runs over.
> - Psalm 23:5

> Surely goodness and mercy
> shall follow me all the days of my life,
> and I shall dwell
> in the house of the LORD forever.
> - Psalm 23:6

Even knowing all this, I lived imprisoned by my mind. I lived the silent struggle. Until I came to the realization that struggles are the setup for successes! I finally understood that I could not change everything I faced, but I could change nothing if I did not face it.

Today, I am at the point where I am so desperate for freedom I have nothing to hide. I don't know the number of guys I have dealt with, sexually and non-sexually, how many apps I've downloaded only to delete out of guilt or after I'd gained what I felt would suffice, how many relationships with godly women I've turned down because I was afraid I would destroy them. I often pray, asking God why I face this torment, why I can't struggle like a normal guy.

Have you ever wondered why Jesus picked Judas? Sometimes the Judas in your life does more for your destiny than you realize. It is not always the good things that show who you are; it is sometimes the horrible people and experiences that God uses to show you what you are made of. Keep pressing on, even when the difficulties arise, even when they escalate.

Often, when I prayed, it seemed the struggles became worse. I couldn't understand until I began to read about Paul's life in the Bible and peruse his letter to the newly established Christian Church. Paul tells readers of "a thorn in the flesh" which he continually prayed God would remove from his life, but instead God repeatedly told Paul, "My grace is sufficient for you. My strength is made perfect in your weakness."

No one knows what Paul's "thorn in the flesh" was, though many have speculated it was a physical ailment or a person who continually persecuted Paul. And while we don't know the details, it was obviously something difficult or even impossible to resolve, whether it was spiritual, physical, or emotional. The "thorn in the flesh" was a struggle for Paul, a battle if you will, like the inner demons we all face at one time or another.

Paul, rather than give up, continued to pray to God, who often intervened on his behalf, in the same way He intervenes on our behalf today. Like Paul, we must be willing to throw all our cards on the table before God and man, while staying strong in our faith and wisdom, knowing that God is always with us.

Out of the Pit

You might feel like Joseph, imprisoned in a pit, left for dead, with no consciousness of God's favor on you. And yet, at the end of the day, God's favor is on you, in both the good times when it is obvious, and the bad times when you can't fathom His presence.

The essential point is, you cannot determine His favor by your circumstances. If you have His favor, it is upon you whether it looks like it or feels like it. If you feel His favor has left you, take some time and watch God turn around and pull you up from whatever circumstances you find yourself embedded in at the moment. God possesses the ability to use you in any situation you are in, whether you believe it or not. He will use you along with the dreams He has given you for your life.

It is completely irrelevant if your family understands, if your brothers are jealous—God is still going to carry out His plan for your life. Joseph was in a pit, left for dead, and God proclaimed He was still going to use Joseph just as He said. What happened? Joseph's life was one wild roller-coaster ride, complete with high peaks, hair-raising twists and hairpin turns, and some super low points, but all the while God was preparing Joseph and balancing his life to carry out His plan.

As we go forward, today, I challenge you to dream again. Dream outside the scope of past experiences, hardships, tough disappointments, personal shortcomings, self-doubt, confusion, and struggles. I dare you—dream again! Look beyond the surface, above the glass ceilings, the labels and limitations you have placed upon yourself. What do you see? What do you feel?

Can you see and feel God's favor despite your doubts, fears, struggles, and failures? I can wait while you look inside yourself, because in all likelihood, what you are seeing might just be blowing your mind! When you begin to dream again, you have the ability to tap into a realm outlined and overflowing with purpose, designed with the fabric of hope and awash in endless possibilities—God's plan for your life.

Don't stop dreaming, don't stop believing, and never lose hope. Dreams are powerful because they permit your escape from the confinement and structure placed upon you by others, but most importantly, dreaming allows you to escape the very confinement you have placed upon yourself.

I challenge you to dream again, hope again, believe again. I dare you to continue to pursue your dreams with all your heart, breathe, and strength.

Dreams are powerful because they have the ability to affect not only you personally, but those who are around and beside you. There is something about a dream that gives you the ability to tap into who you are destined to be, your full potential. Your dreams present the revelation of your lineage, a royal, aristocratic dynasty, part of God's family and the recipient of His favor.

And one thing we must keep in mind is the goal of the enemy is to make you wonder who you are, why you are here, and force you to forget God has a plan for you. The funny thing about humans is we all possess the ability to dream, and the only person who can hinder your dreams is you! I have learned in this world you have to be careful when you open yourself to the influence and opinion of others. If you fall under their influence, you may lose yourself, your identity, and find yourself at war between two worlds.

In my own life, I had to discover for myself that my destiny is not predicated by what others think of me and/or the labels they put upon me. I've learned your dreams will cause controversies among those who want to come down on your dream, separating you from your dream, saying your dream is trouble...

Like many of us, some of the most talented, faithful, and amazing people in the Bible didn't realize what they had inside themselves—that is, not until God revealed to them the truth about their identity and abilities. These revelations often came in the midst of perilous trials and challenging situations. Like these heroes of Christianity—Noah who faced the cataclysmic flood, Abraham who was asked by God to leave his country and all he knew to go on God's mission, Sarah to whom God promised to build a nation even though she was past childbearing years and barren, Joseph whose family hated him and sold him into slavery, Moses who was tasked with leading the Israelites out of slavery in Egypt, Rahab who risked her life to help the Israelite spies take the Promised Land, Daniel who was condemned to death in the lion's den, and many more throughout the scriptures, all of us have untapped talents, unclaimed abilities, and unknown gifts waiting to be discovered.

God wants us to peel away the layers we try to hide behind, dissolve the excuses we use as camouflage, and reveal the beauty of our true selves. In Sheryl Brady's book, *You Have It In You!: Empowered to Do the Impossible,* she shares her own life journey as well as examples from history and current culture. Brady encourages each of us to reconsider the way we see ourselves and to reframe our own understanding of how we got there. *You Have It in You!* asks, "Do you know what you're made of? More importantly, do you want to discover the strengths lying dormant inside you?"—all in the hope you will be inspired to view challenges as opportunities for self-discovery and to enrich your faith.

In all honesty, sometimes the devil sets out to destroy you. Past experiences and difficult circumstances make us wonder at God's favor and question our dreams. These are the times when the only way to RISE ABOVE IT is to actually GO THROUGH IT. Bad things happen to good people all the time, but to those who keep the faith, what are a few battle scars when you have the FINAL VICTORY?

Do your past experiences and bad decisions ruin your chance for a better future? Is there any way to know for certain you're on the right track? In reality, God can use both the good and the bad in your life to direct your paths. God doesn't promise to guard you from trouble. He promises to guide you successfully through it.

God is our refuge and strength,
A very present help in trouble.
Therefore we will not fear,
Even though the earth be removed,
And though the mountains be carried
into the midst of the sea.
- Psalms 46:1-2

The opposition you face doesn't prevent the presence of God in your life; instead it proves the presence of God.

Don't allow something or someone to limit you. The limitations you accept can keep you from experiencing the destiny for which you were created. Life isn't equal, but God's grace levels the playing field.

Chapter 4
Growing Pain

Change is never easy. Every day that passes in our lives means we deal with an excess of ambiguity which creates added complexity and makes decision-making even more difficult. In addition, ambiguity creates high levels of uncertainty, stress, and struggle. I never thought for a moment that through all the rejection, abuse, disappointment, and confusion about my personal identity there was still hope for me to find a sense of peace about myself, despite a number of hiccups along the way.

I want you to understand that regardless of your past experiences or your current tribulation, there is still hope for you, for your development, and for your destiny. There is growth in your pain, growth which can give you a new perspective on all God has brought you through and a greater awareness of all you've accomplished and endured. Your present situation is no indication of your future reality!

What we often fail to realize is some people can come alongside you and walk with you through the pain, encouraging and strengthening you, but even so, they cannot go with you to the next level. Though they may know your struggles and your pain, or even share a similar story, they have not experienced it in the same way as you. You still need people who can connect with you, but in reality, less is more. You will never be friends with everyone, but you can be real friends with a select few.

I had few friends growing up, during the time of my abuse and molestation. One of them, Jordan, lived across the street with his mother and grandmother, and we played together all the time— ninja make-believe, bike riding, and all sorts of fun kid games. I felt safe at his house, but it was at the house of my other friend that I learned what a family should be like. My other childhood friend, Anthony, lived with his mom and dad. When I was at his house, I truly felt I was safe and secure, spending time with a real family. Anthony's mom and dad laughed together, cooked together, had dinner together, and even went on dates with each other. His family did almost everything together—from the mundane, like watching television, to the exciting, like going on a vacation. It was truly like nothing I had ever experienced.

At my house, everyone grabbed their dinner plate and headed to their rooms to eat. Sometimes my dad was there; other times, he disappeared for weeks. When my dad was home, no one knew if he would come through the door as our dad or the angry and bellowing man with the drug and alcohol problems. I lived in fear of my father most of the time—afraid of the man who had the power to release and strengthen my true identity.

And then there were the friends and neighbors all around us, but even though they knew our "dirty little secrets," no one talked about it or intervened on our behalf when the abuse occurred. Of course, there were also the "friends" of my siblings who often stayed at our house, one of whom eventually molested me at eleven years old. And with that, I'd like to remind you—there is a thin line between a parasite and a friend!

Raw Materials

Raw materials, by definition, can be natural resources or processed material which are converted in production or manufacturing into a new and useful product. For people, something similar can be said. As human beings we have natural abilities, talents, and gifts, which are unique to us but can be transformed into powerful new characteristics, talents, and abilities.

Think about it: like me, you have perseverance, you have determination. You have the ability to focus and work hard. You have hopes and dreams for your life. If you are like most of us, you have had doors open for you and had other doors close. You have not let that stop you in the pursuit of your dreams, but instead looked for another chance, another opportunity. Each of these are great qualities—raw materials, if you will.

Life does not always happen the way you hope it will, but still, there are many more doors waiting to open in your life. You simply have to keep using your "raw materials" to find them. You may have to leap, climb, or step over those obstacles that arise in your path—every day!

The truth is, you, like me, are stronger than you think...you can conquer the obstacles, despite your shortcomings—real or imagined. You and I can impact, influence, and redefine life—our own lives and the lives of others.

Everything we face, on a daily basis, is an experience, not THE EXPERIENCE. We each face our own set of growing pains as we develop, walk forward, face setbacks, and wait. There are times when we must even close a door to grow.

One important lesson I have learned as I continue to grow is if you don't need God to help you accomplish your goal, then in all likelihood, God is not in it and never was! And in those times, I often get lost in my thoughts and wonder what God sees in me. Why on earth would God take an insecure guy from the northwest side of Detroit, who was abused, used, rejected, and molested? A boy who, as a child, was labeled retarded? A child with a speech impediment?

And then, I understand, and I sit and thank God for isolating me from the world around me, raising me to stand against injustice and stand for equality. Many of the situations and circumstances I dealt with weren't about me in that moment. Instead, they were about positioning me in the place where I could be effective in serving others, motivating, mentoring, inspiring, and helping to heal.

Remember, you and I have the power of choice. We can't control every situation or every circumstance, but we can control how we respond. Remember the "perspective" makes all the difference, and it is up to us to "respect the steps."

Respect the Steps

One day while I was watching *Scandal*, Fitz was teaching Olivia the importance of forgiveness; not only about forgiving others, but also forgiving oneself. In that moment, I was also being taught the importance of forgiveness.

You have to climb out. You need a line.
A rationale. A story you can tell yourself.
Doesn't matter what it is. Doesn't even have to be true.
So long as you believe it.
So long as it allows you to forgive yourself.
Find that line. That purpose. Find it.
You can do that. I know you can.
Find it. Grab hold of it.
And use it to pull yourself up and out of the darkness.
- Fitzgerald Grant

Let's begin by remembering your past life is too small to fit you as you grow into the fullness of the individual you were meant to be. Henry David Thoreau once stated, "If one advances confidently in the direction of his dreams, and endeavors to live the life which he has imagined, he will meet with a success unexpected in common hours." This is true, but it requires, in many instances, that we grow through our pain.

In all honesty, the more FUNCTIONAL you become, the greater the number of DYSFUNCTIONAL situations that pop up in your life. Try to remain focused on your dreams and the life you have imagined for yourself, without getting too frustrated—after all, it is just a way to build more character and process your raw materials.

There are principles, philosophies, and ideas in your life you believe because you have been taught they are true, but there are other beliefs, views, and ideas you know for certain, because you have lived, strived, tried, and found they have proven themselves to be true. Apply that truth, and don't kill yourself trying to accomplish all by yourself, but understand the right people will show up at the right time.

> A friend loves at all times,
> and a brother is born
> for adversity.
> - Proverbs 17:17 ESV

In all situations and circumstances, never lose your desire to be inspired. If you do, you are living in the wrong circle. You need to make a change, respect the steps, and live to be inspired so you can inspire before you expire.

Often, if you change your perspective, you can completely change what productivity looks like in your life and how quickly your dreams can be accomplished. The goal is to move from Should...

To Would...

To Could...

To Done!!!

This issue is personal for me. As I have grown, I have come to understand I must be determined to be hopeful in order to be empowered. I pray on a daily basis, "Lord, take my nothing and turn it into something amazing." I have discovered the very thing which makes me different is the very thing that makes me special—and the same is true for you as well!

As you realize this truth, keep in mind you cannot try to please everyone; no one will be pleased, and you will be full of regrets. Add the responsibility to carry on your family's legacy in a positive way, and you'll find that nothing is ever perfect.

To handle these pressures and the pain that often accompanies them, I have come to understand I am a prize to be won, and knowing that truth means I can refuse to settle for less than God's best for me! My insight on this topic came from an unexpected source, one completely out of the blue—my father. The year was 2004, and my father was finally getting himself together, coming to a place of pride for me, as he sent me off to college—the first in my family. My mother had only then told him of my molestation by my elder brother, Malik, as well as our family friend.

I was in the shower of our family home when my father walked in without warning. I had just wrapped my towel around me when he hugged me, crying, and said, "You are my son. You are a man. Your body is a gift. You only give gifts to those you love. You do not share your gift with everyone, because everyone is not deserving of that gift."

My father spoke with such power and conviction I immediately comprehended the depth of his feelings. It was truly a breakthrough, and our long-lost father-son relationship began its restoration that day. It was the day he became my dad again, once more my champion.

Later that day, my father confessed to me he was glad Malik was currently in prison, because he felt his anger at what had happened knew no bounds. My dad thought he might have killed Malik, for hurting his "baby boy." Honestly, those words, calling me his "baby," were the first affectionate reference I had ever heard from my father. My dad became very protective of me that day and every day that followed until his death, which came later that year. I often wonder if his anger, regret, and guilt played a role in his passing.

From my dad that day I learned this truth: your gift may carry you to places where your character cannot keep you. It is important here, and I know this to be the absolute truth from my own personal experience, that I tell you to STOP looking for answers in all the wrong places.

You have a destiny and in view of that destiny, you must run your race. Your race will be challenging, but if it does not challenge you, then it will not better you! Remember, God does not make mistakes, and He is not about to start with you.

There will always be conflict between the ordinary and the exceptional. The people and the circumstances around you may try to define you as ordinary, but there is much about you they do not know (and you may not even know yourself—YET), and you are exceptional. In light of that fact, I would like to serve notice to the voices, external and internal, that would try to limit what God is promoting in you.

Never let someone else's history keep you from your own promising future. You do not have to know where you are going to distance yourself from your used-to-be! God has a plan for you and for me, and he wants us to respect the steps and run the race he sets before us.

Each of us has a story the world needs to hear. There is more to life, and there is always something bigger than you—but you have a history of overcoming disappointments, obstacles, difficulties, and trials. There is a giant with your name on it, just like Goliath was standing before David, and that giant will only fall when you tap into your spiritual inheritance!

Are you ready? God is forcing your faith to stretch, so you will grow! He wants you to be a blank canvas, so He can fill in the gaps! You always have victory when you remember God is on your side.

Ask God to supply your new normal for no other reason than your destiny thrives off the *Spirit of the Living God*! God uses transformation, growth, and even sometimes pain to manifest His plan for your life. It begins with you asking God to do it and listening for His answer and following His direction. He is always saying you can become it, because it is already done!

Whether you see it or not, the bigger the obstacle...the bigger the victory! You never have to be afraid or uncertain of the outcome because God reminds us over and over in His Word, the battle is not ours—the battle belongs to the Lord.

Thus, says the LORD to you, "Do not be afraid and do not be dismayed at this great horde, for the battle is not yours but God's."
- 2 Chronicles 20:15b

*****

Fear not, stand firm, and see the salvation of the LORD, which He will work for you today. For the Egyptians whom you see today, you shall never see again. The LORD will fight for you, and you have only to be silent.
- Exodus 14:13-14

*****

And that all this assembly may know that the LORD saves not with sword and spear.
For the battle is the LORD's,
and he will give you into our hand.
- I Samuel 17:47

These are only a few samples of God's declaration that our battles are not our own, but His—so are you ready now to make an I.M.P.A.C.T?

Making an I.M.P.A.C.T

Be Intentional
In Genesis 50:20, Joshua speaks the words to the brothers who betrayed him and left him for dead, "You intended to harm me, but God intended it all for good. He brought me to this position so I could save the lives of many people." Whether you see it or not, the bigger the obstacle in your way... the bigger the victory awaiting you! You never have to be afraid or uncertain of the outcome because as God has already promised, the battle is not yours—the battle belongs to the Lord. All you have to do is be intentional and show up.

Movement

In Genesis 1:2, God relates this scenario to Moses, who records it for us: "The earth was formless and void, and darkness was over the surface of the deep, and the Spirit of God was moving over the surface of the waters." Movement requires motion, a step in the right direction. God is ready to change, move, and shift something in your life. ARE YOU READY TO MAKE THAT MOVE? Remember you must make the decision to move and follow up with a single step...

Produce

In the beginning, God had a lot to say about producing. In Genesis 1:11, "God said, 'Let the earth **produce** vegetation: seed-bearing plants, and fruit trees on the earth bearing fruit with seed in it, according to their kinds.' And it was so." A short while later, in Genesis 1:24, "God said, 'Let the earth **produce** living creatures according to their kinds: livestock, creatures that crawl, and the wildlife of the earth according to their kinds.' And it was so." And right after that, in Genesis 1:29, "God also told them (Adam and Eve, 'Look! I have given you every seed-bearing plant that grows throughout the earth, along with every tree that grows seed-bearing fruit. They will **produce** your food.'"

Obviously, God's raw materials produce a great product. Most people concern themselves with the outcome of the raw materials—the product—rather than considering the raw material. The raw materials serve a purpose, and without them, there is no final product. In our case, we are God's raw materials and he is molding, shaping, and growing us into His finished product.

Action

In Philippians 4:13, Paul, under the inspiration of the Holy Spirit, proclaims, "I can **do** all things through Christ who strengthens me." Like Paul, with God's Spirit, you have it in you as well! You have what it takes to spring into action and be victorious because you are "fearfully and wonderfully made"—set apart by God and uniquely equipped for action.

Continuous

Are you like me? I have a structured mind. I like things in order. I like things to be black and white. But over the years, I have learned life isn't that way. Early in my career, I struggled with understanding exactly what my responsibilities would be. With my personality, as you can imagine, I wanted it to be clear—black and white. My boss reminded me, "...in a senior position, you have to deal with ambiguity." Though at the time, the feedback hurt a bit, I realized he was right.

In spite of the ambiguity we are faced with daily, we must continue to move forward in our quest for our dreams and the life we have imagined. God tells us in the book of Hebrews, chapter 10, verses 35 and 36, "Do not throw away this confident trust in the Lord, no matter what happens. Remember the great reward it brings you! Patient endurance is what you need now, so you will continue to do God's will. Then you will receive all that he has promised." And with those words, we should be inspired to continue confidently following the path He has placed before us in our lives.

Transformation

In Romans 12:2, we are instructed, "Do not conform to the pattern of this world but be transformed by the renewing of your mind. Then you will be able to test and approve what God's will is— His good, pleasing, and perfect will." This transformation doesn't come from inspiration; rather, transformation takes place in your mind. Transformation is all-encompassing and requires us to seriously examine what ails us, what we are struggling against, and how to overcome. It is the transformation of our mindset in order to gain a better understanding.

In the natural world, hosts of animals undergo a metamorphosis, changing all aspects of themselves to better adapt to their environment. Similarly, our own metamorphosis awaits. When you change the way you think, you can change your life! You can now understand the importance of growth in spite of pain, the significance of going forward, following God's guidance into a brighter future, and the importance of change, transforming yourself into all God has planned for you. Not everyone will understand your desire to transform, but that is okay. It is not their journey to understand—it is yours!

Chapter 5
What Are You Fighting For?
(It is Up to Us to Fight Back)

Countless times I have asked myself what I am fighting for. I've hoped to discover my motives and objectives. Instead, I have ultimately wound up convinced there are others waiting for me to become my best self so they can, in turn, become their best selves. Once I arrived at the place of seeing beyond my own personal opposition, I came to understand the importance of finding myself so I might help others through the process.

No, I don't yet know all the answers throughout this process called life, but I do understand the importance of unity. I have come to comprehend the importance of having someone encourage you along the way. And so, the message I want to deliver is to encourage you. No matter what you are going through in this moment, you must keep fighting. We must come to an understanding of the appropriate time to fight, regardless of the circumstances, and continue our quest until we win.

Trusting God in Difficult Times

No matter the battles you face, your situation, or your circumstances—past or present—you need to dream again, to believe again, to hope again. Despite all the challenges you have gone through, you have overcome everyone who failed you, everyone who walked out of your life. The fact that you have come through this means you are a fighter who has survived. Your fight is the fix, and you will come out of it victorious—stronger than ever before.

The thing is, we must fight—for ourselves—regardless of how tired we are or how defeated we feel; we must carry on and continue the battle. This fight is not only about us, but about all those who come after us. We must fight regardless of what people say and do, regardless of how we feel—because there are individuals depending on us!

In all our struggles, it is God who validates us. Contrary to what modern society would have you believe, our validation does not come via social media, nor our peers; it is not from our church, nor is it from our followers.

The Fight to Your Destiny

What is the size of your storm?

If it's a big storm; then you have a big call and a big promise. More importantly, you have the ability to get through it!

Get ready to hit refresh on your story, your journey, and your life. Turn your storm into an unshakable relationship with God and a ministry that touches people's lives.

-Cora Jakes Coleman

You are too close to the finish line to stop now. Even though there are those waiting to see you fail, there are more counting on you to win. Your destiny, your future, your purpose, starts RIGHT NOW! You must make the decision. Are you going to live today being THE BEST YOU?

Keep in mind, your opposition is your opportunity because the ordinary is intimidated by the extraordinary. You need to conquer what you keep quitting. Once you do, you will finish what you started. In the fight, you need to appreciate the fact that your voice is distinct and powerful, your voice is necessary in God's plan, your voice matters.

God demonstrates this truth in nature. An eagle does not concern himself with the troubles on the ground. No matter how disappointing or dangerous the situation looks on the ground beneath him, the eagle never panics. He simply does what God created him to do—rise above the circumstances.

The truth is, this kind of trust in God does not happen when life appears to be perfect. Trust in God is developed when everything appears to be falling apart at the seams and nothing seems to be working out. Trusting God happens when circumstances seem to be beating you down, but you keep standing and continue fighting. Not only do you continue to stand and fight, but all the while you manage to maintain a good attitude because you know God has your back in ALL things.

I would like to make this very clear: even though there are times when I cannot see my way, I still trust God. One such time, when I was compelled to fight, was my senior year of college. I was entering my final year at Alabama State University when I found myself under the evaluation of clinical psychologists in Montgomery, Alabama.

I was twenty-one years old at the time, and while I had made some strides forward, I was still struggling with my past as well as my sexuality. The initial evaluation was intended to determine any learning disabilities or attentional issues, with the final report to be sent to Alabama State Department of Special Education Services.

The initial observations and history were recorded as follows:

- 21 years old
- African-American
- Well-groomed
- 6' tall, 120 lbs.
- Able to provide social security number and birthdate without written reference
- Reported heart murmur and heart palpitations (I told them "my heart speeds up sometimes.")
- Evident speech difficulties
- Denied issues with alcohol or drugs, no current medication
- No previous treatment by mental health professionals
- Denied attention deficit disorder
- Reported previous learning disabilities diagnoses

- Mother, living; Father, deceased, myocardial infarction; two brothers, living; one sister, living

At the time, I lived on campus with three roommates. I had just completed my third year of college, and I was majoring in Business Administration and holding a GPA of 3.0. My most recent ACT score was 11. I also had an on-campus job. I tell you all of this, so you can understand exactly where I was when I received what I felt was a devastating diagnosis. And more importantly so you, no matter what your circumstances or situation, can fight as I did against what seemed an impossible battle.

The examination began with a number of questions which I strove to answer honestly and patiently. No, I did not have sleep issues. No, I did not have crying spells. No, I did not experience hallucinations or delusions. No, I did not have suicidal intent, nor had I ever attempted suicide. According to the expert examining me, my recall of general information was poor and my memory was clouded. In addition, I was unable to do serial subtractions from one hundred.

Other testing scores seemed equally disappointing to me, but I was here for help, so I persevered through the entire battery of testing. My perseverance was rewarded with this assessment by the examining psychologist. "On the WAIS-111, Danarius generated a Verbal IQ of 68, a Performance IQ of 63, and a Full-Scale IQ of 63, placing him in the mild range of mental retardation at the present time relative to his same age peers. His task performance was quite consistent and low with no areas of strength or weakness. There was no evidence on any of the test results to suggest the presence of focal organic pathology or malingering. The results of achievement testing show that this individual is currently reading and spelling with standard scores of 70 and 60 respectively. He has minimal literacy skills in both of these areas." Additionally, there came the diagnosis of "Mild Mental Retardation."

The doctor's recommendation read as follows: "This patient does not appear to have a learning disability or attention deficit problems. **He does not belong in college. He simply will not be able to utilize college material in order to be employed at the college level.** He may have some assets which would sustain him for training at the technical school or junior college level, but the examiner doubts even that."

As ironic as this all was, given that I was entering my senior year of college with a 3.0 average, I was devastated. Like many black men entering college, I

carried the hopes and dreams of my family and my community. Like them, I aspired to become someone, in business, healthcare, entertainment, technology, or the law—a successful professional. Many of these men go on to graduate and achieve their dreams; for others the dreams become nightmares.

To Be or Not to Be – A Statistic

After this diagnosis, I had to choose—fight or give up. The American Psychiatric Association reports that on average five to ten percent of black men In college suffer from depression on campus related to isolation, discrimination, or stress. In 2015, the National College Health Assessment reported eighteen percent of students stated depression negatively affected their ability to fulfill required college functions, while *Science Daily* reports that students suffering from depression are twice as likely to become college dropouts.

What do you fight for?
I fight for the ones in my corner,
for the ones that lift me up.
I fight for the things that matter,
for my family, for my friends and
for the ones I love.
I know what I fight for.
- Michael B. Jordan in *Creed*

What would I do? Fight! I knew I could cope with adversity—I had done it my entire life. The difficulty would come in embracing my self-worth, something I still struggle with today.

I never thought, even for a moment or in my wildest dreams, that by the age of thirty-one, I would be where I am today. To be young, black, educated, and employed. I discovered early on that "Young, Black, and Educated" was not just a slogan on the front of my shirt, but rather a way of life for me.

I have said to myself many times over the course of my life, "I must be doing something right, right?" For so long, I utilized church, work, and education to hide and or to distract me from my issues, or more specifically, from dealing with my struggles.

This lasted until December 17, 2016, supposedly the greatest day of my life (no, I did not get married or have a baby) when I finally received my doctorate, yet also the day my whole world came crashing down. It was the day I learned "Monopoly" is not only a board game, but a depiction of real life. It was the day I realized I did not have the option of passing go and collecting $200, but I did have the option of addressing and facing the adversity in my life.

Have you ever tried to trick yourself into believing something in your life was not truly reality? I found myself asking, "What adversity are you talking about?" Then, I found myself asking, "What are you afraid of facing?" So, the questions made me think. "Am I afraid of success? Am I afraid of commitment? Am I afraid of relationships? Am I afraid of being alone?" The answer was always "no," because I know exactly what I am afraid of...

I talked to myself a lot. Everything I feared and tried to avoid came rushing in like a flood. I thought I had mastered the art of avoiding the adversity in my mind. Instead, a thousand and one thoughts started to flood my mind as I began to explore my deepest fears.

Nevertheless, the question came: "What do you do when you come to a fork in the road?" Clearly, you do not pass go, and you do not to collect $200; rather, you face your adversity head-on!

I am often still haunted by the idea that I am not good enough, and that is when I remind myself of The Five E's of Coping with Adversity while embracing your self-worth.

Adversity teaches you that you are stronger than you ever thought. Have you ever found yourself in a struggle . . . a trial . . . a battle? Everyone has; you are not alone. But, more importantly, are you in one now? A financial battle? A fight for your health? A struggle to save your marriage? A battle for your child or grandchild?

Regardless of the battle you are facing, the Five Essential Elements (5 Es) for Dealing and Coping with Adversity will set you on the path to overcome your adversity.

1. **Evaluate / Envision** - You are NOT defined by your situation. You are the architect of your own dreams; now is the time to envision and begin building one brick at a time. It is often the journey which teaches us about the destination.
2. **Engage** – You must take over your mindset regardless of what you've been through. Your mindset does not determine the outcome of your life.
3. **Exit Strategy** - Be prepared to fight for yourself. Don't wait for someone to fight for you!
4. **Evolve and Transform the Way You Think** - If we truly want to change the future, then we need to learn from our past.
5. **Experience Fullness of Peace and Freedom** - You don't have to fight in your own strength, because the battle is not yours . . . the battle is the Lord's!

Each of our stories, yours and mine, can be great once we learn to delve beneath the surface and see our own depth. We cannot let negativity hold us back from giving our best every day. We must strive to "give it all we've got!" on a daily basis.

My strength comes from lifting myself up when I was knocked down. It meant I had to learn to drop the masks and stop auditioning people in my bed to find myself. I am no longer a victim; I am a winner, and I utilize that fact to strengthen myself.

Mistakes are simply a fact of life. It is our response to the errors that makes all the difference in our lives and who we become. There are times when it seems God allows us to go through hell on Earth in order to reveal the depths of His love for us. As we learn from the apostle Paul, we must not despise the thorn—it is teaching us something.

...I was given a thorn in my flesh, a messenger of Satan, to torment me. Three times I pleaded with the Lord to take it away from me. But He said to me, "My grace is sufficient for you, for my power is made perfect in weakness."

Therefore, I will boast all the more gladly about my weaknesses, so that Christ's power may rest on me.

That is why, for Christ's sake, I delight in weaknesses, in insults, in hardships, in persecutions, in difficulties.

For when I am weak, then I am strong."
- 2 Corinthians 12:7b-10

You may have to fight a battle more than once to win it. Understand, your fight is not over yet. Believe there will be a clearing in the trees. You are coming out of the woods. Be encouraged, it will get better.

I have come to understand that with every obstacle, we can overcome with confidence if we choose to stand and fight:

- How do you face molestation? You face it head-on!
- How do you face an identity issue? You face it head-on!

- How do you face rejection and disappointment? You face it head-on!
- How do you face physical, mental, and emotional abuse? You face it head-on!

Facing and overcoming adversity can become one of your biggest advantages, as long as you understand at some point you must forgive yourself for carrying the weight of the adversity you have overcome. At no time do we have the option of avoidance.

My story is already written. I know, now, it is not the size of the challenges, but your view of the challenges in the light of who you know God to be, which determines your odds of victory. The greatest enemy of our destiny is complacency.

God's Power and His People

Don't underestimate God's power to use people to lead you to the right place—the place He wants you to be—ultimately the place of His favor. Often, we expect God's will to be revealed through a specific Bible verse, in the form of a spiritual impression or a dream. But what if God wants to speak into your life through a person who is right in front of you?

Your destiny is the deliberate fulfillment of a divine purpose, at God's divinely appointed time. It is ahead of you—it is your time! Even when God allows the naysayers to say differently, look to Jesus! There is always opportunity in opposition. You have to fight, remembering joy and depression cannot occupy the same space.

One of the greatest challenges in life is discovering who you are; the second greatest is being happy with what you find. We must reevaluate our priorities and watch for God's power and His people in our lives.

I am sharing this with you because I care. I know better than to trust speculations and good intentions. I want us to look out for each other. Each of us needs to fight for our lives and our rights.

Now more than ever, you need to get involved and fight like hell alongside us, otherwise, we will lose everything.

In this day and age, I have learned you have to fight for your purpose, your destiny, and also your peace of mind, because if you don't, you stand a chance of losing it all. Bishop T.D. Jakes stated, "Don't stop at where you are as if it were the destination, when in fact, in reality, it may be the transportation that brings you into that thing you were created to do."

This is just a reminder that our current circumstances, opposition, and/or adversity should never limit us from reaching our true potential. This is why we are so critical to this equation, because it allows us the opportunity to learn from each other while utilizing our shortcomings, our adversity, and our struggles as a tool of transportation to help us to get to our final destination of a total transformation.

Everything we have ever experienced or gone through is preparation for our destiny, for what is about to happen in our lives, and where God is about to take us.

Have you ever wondered where we would be if Dr. Martin Luther King, Jr. never marched on Washington? Or if Barbara Rose Johns, the girl who sparked Brown v. Board of Education, never stood up for students' opportunity for equal education? Or even if Harry Potter never had the audacity to take on Voldemort, because he didn't know how to deal with the loss of his parents? What if Hillary Clinton never tried to break every glass ceiling, giving women everywhere the encouragement that they can do and become anything? Where would we be in the hour of adversity? In reality, adversity is just a state of mind. It's only a minute or second—it's not meant to last a lifetime or season. Just like autumn leaves wither and fall, adversity, too, will come and go. It is hard to imagine that adversity could be an advantage, but it can be:

- Adversity is an opportunity.
- Adversity is an opportunity for resilience.
- Adversity is an opportunity for change.

- Adversity is an opportunity for growth.

Of course, I fight to live every day, because I trust His plan for my life. He knew the day I would be born and He knows the date of my death. I am going to live life to the fullest and die contented and loved, whenever that time comes.

Fighting harder will not change the outcome God has in store for me or you. Even so, I will never give up the day-to-day fight to stay positive, to love and glorify God.

Becoming a Warrior with a Purpose

This brings up another question...what kind of warrior are you? There are those on the front line who go in guns blazing, or who charge in with hand-to-hand combat. They have their comrades surrounding them and the battle plan is laid out. I love this type of person—they are strong warriors. A warrior is not afraid to die, or they would never go into battle.

There are others, like me, who are only strong and courageous because they have to be. I, personally, am not any stronger than anyone else in this situation. Most of the time I feel weak, confused, insecure, and vulnerable. God is the one who is strong, not me.

It is here we must strengthen ourselves with our girdle of truth, covering the weak places. Trouble knows your weakness, so stop telegraphing it. As long as we fail to cover our weak spots, we are telegraphing to the enemy where our weaknesses are, and we know the enemy is opportunistic. If he knows where our weakness is, then that is where he will attack.

So, in declaring this war against evil, trouble, and adversity, we understand we must expect a fight. It is already written in His Word that we win, so we must fight with mastery in mind. Remember speaking things into existence and sowing and reaping did not come from *The Secret's* "Law of Attraction." The fact is, we can call things to ourselves, good and bad—this was and always will be God's design of free will and individual choices. It is not a "Universe" design or something set in place by chance or anything other than the Sovereign God, who called light out of darkness and spoke the creation into existence. The law of reciprocity was set in place by God when He said, "While the Earth remains, seed time and harvest shall not cease" (Genesis 8:22). God is Spirit, and He put this law in place in the spiritual realm and the natural realm.

Even our casual conversation needs to bring us what we desire and not destruction. You have authority over your words. Am I saying be all spooky with it? No, of course not, but I am saying when you truly begin to CHOOSE your words, you will really CHANGE your life.

Stop dancing around the truth. Set your feet in what is right and hold your position. If the fight does not call for the use of faith, then it is not the good fight of faith. Whatever battle we choose to fight, we must apply faith, or it is not a fight in which we should be engaged.

If you truly believe that without faith it is impossible to please God, then you would come vocally against anything which attacks your faith or causes your faith to waver. Don't stand idle and allow the attack; choose how you will fight.

It Is Fight Day!

So, what are we fighting for? Are we fighting to stay out of sin? Are we fighting to stay in sin? Are we fighting to stay in darkness? Are we fighting to stay in light?

Everyone is fighting something, but what are you fighting for? Why fight each other when you have chosen the wrong person to fight? Why kill each other when you have chosen the wrong target? Why hate each other when you have selected the wrong person to hate? Why sabotage each other when the person targeted has caused you no harm? Why think evil of one another when the people have done no evil against you? Have you not read that we are not fighting against flesh and blood?

If you want to fight the right target, fight the devil and his evil angels. If you want to kill someone, kill your flesh, so you can follow Jesus. In the battle, you must fight against the "demons" that plague you—only then can you grow into the amazing person God has planned for you to become. Fight against self-judgement and instead apply an accurate reflection of yourself—the one God has for you. If you want to think evil of someone, think evil of the devil, the master of evil. Think evil of him because he wants to spread his wicked thoughts and ideas about you to you to keep you down. Don't allow it. Fight the battle to your best self, and never surrender.

So, again I ask, what are you fighting for? Are you fighting to stand strong and be the person God intends you to be in His kingdom? Or have you thrown your towel in?

We are in a spiritual battle! And the question is, "Who is on the Lord's side?" Either you are, or you are not—there is NO in between. Make sure your fight is against the kingdom of darkness and the evil attacks perpetrated against you to hold you down and keep you from God's purposes and His victories in your life.

And be encouraged by the words of the Lord.

But he that shall endure unto the end, the same shall be saved.

- Matthew 24:13

*****

Thou therefore endure hardness, as a good soldier of Jesus Christ.

- 2 Timothy 2:3

*****

For we wrestle not against flesh and blood,
but against principalities, against powers,

against the rulers of the darkness of this world,
against spiritual wickedness in high places.
Wherefore take unto you the whole armour of God,
that ye may be able to withstand in the evil day,
and having done all, to stand.
- Ephesians 6:12-13

The Victors

There is no doubt in my mind that those who are on the Lord's side are the victors and no longer the victims. The victors in God's kingdom are of self-confidence, self-worth, and reliance on God—knowing nothing is impossible with God. Never let OUTSIDE circumstances dictate your INNER peace!

Our greatest battle will always be fought at the door of our greatest opportunity. It is important to remember God will always have the last word. Don't ever tell a problem to people who can't solve it, but rather give your problems over to the one who can—God! There are times when God will let you experience the seemingly impossible, so you can know nothing is impossible with God. Not only is God in the outcome, but He is also in the part you don't like!

When people desert you...God is there! Remember, you are not limited by people's low expectations, but you are propelled by God's promises. Our fate, yours and mine, is not in the hands of chance; it is in our hands and we must not wait for it, we must embrace it. Those who want to achieve great things must dig deep, make sharp decisions, think outside the box, and hold their ground. When you are doing your best to do the right thing, life-changing things, don't let anyone tell you to stop.

The attacks on your life have much more to do with who you can be in the future than who you have been in the past. The enemy fears you are becoming the man or woman God has designed you to be. Don't judge when you only have half of the story. Greatness doesn't always come packaged as greatness.

Chapter 6
Pressure Prepares You for Purpose

Like me, YOU are here to make a difference! The thing is, we often stand in our own way. We have to keep the pressure on—because the fight we find ourselves in is one we must win. It is time to show our strength and identify what we are truly fighting for—our life's purpose.

I don't want to wait anymore; I don't want to miss achieving my purpose. I must do something now, even if that means running toward the very thing that terrifies me! When you are in doubt, you must never run away. You have to stand in the doorway and walk through it confidently. This may mean moving on, leaving behind those who are holding you back.

So far, you have heard bits and pieces of my story; here I would like to share how mentors can truly make a difference in life, helping us face the pressure and find our purpose.

More of the Story

I can recall being a youngster growing up in the city of Detroit. From an early age, I began dealing with the pressures of life which sprang from low self-esteem, a result of mental and physical abuse. I felt as if I had no identity, no real connection. The idea of being successful in life was foreign to me due to the nature of my culture and climate.

Until one day, I was given the opportunity to be in the company of two amazing counselors—mentors who possessed the magic and capability of pushing me from my uncomfortable comfort zone and into the commitment zone. They each had the ability to see inside of me to the successful person I could be, but could not yet see.

We formed a bond, student and mentors, a bond that impacted me as the mentee and equipped me to endure. They demonstrated to me the truth that regardless of my life experiences, my limitations (those placed on me by myself or others), my economic status, or my ZIP code, there is always room to grow and to be influenced in positive ways. In turn, this growth and influence eventually gave me the ability to positively impact others.

I was a senior in high school when these two counselors began to crack my shell, forcing me to begin the evolution of the person I am today. From that point forward, teachers began to pour into my life, helping me develop socially, morally, and spiritually. This was the initial step toward my understanding and accepting that I had a heart for people.

We had to look at the residue which remained from the molestation I'd experienced. They understood and helped me identify not only with the fact of it, but also with the aftermath of being molested. It was not easy.

In this day and age, we have many laws, regulations, and policies in effect. These laws range from freedom of speech to the right to bear arms. The purpose of these laws, regulations, and policies is to protect individuals, from harm and danger. These laws were established because the people understood the importance of protection.

Everyone has the desire to be protected from one thing or another, yet all our fears are different. For example, wives often look to their husbands to be protectors and providers. Children look to their parents to be protectors and providers. Civilians look to their local police department and armed services as their protectors. If we do our research and examine what took place from a historical and Biblical standpoint, we will see similar examples, generations of people looking for a protector, or in many cases, a deliverer.

In my case, as an adolescent, I can remember being a fan of superheroes. A superhero is a character possessing "extraordinary or superhuman powers" who is dedicated to protecting the public. I always looked to those I believed were stronger than me to protect me. I didn't quite understand how to protect myself and/or stand up for myself because throughout my life I have dealt with so many conflicts and failures.

As I mentioned earlier, as an African-American boy growing up in Detroit, I found it hard to find my identity and self-worth in a household filled with large measures of abuse, drug addiction, molestation, and mental anguish. As a child raised in the church, this led me to wonder at God and His presence in my life. After all, I was taught weekly that He loved me, and that led me to question this truth as well as ask Him point-blank, "Why me?" It wasn't until years later I would truly get a response.

As the youngest of four children from the union of the late Josiah Hemphill and Laila Smith Hemphill, I was born on September 20, 1985 at Hutzel Hospital. From birth, it appeared the enemy sought me out and formulated a plan to gain the upper hand in my life, thwarting God's purpose for me.

As I have shared, at birth my lungs weren't fully developed. In addition, I had a heart murmur, which would later provide a means for my future success. As I grew, my five-year-old self, innocent and unknowing, witnessed drug abuse (by the man who was my "champion") and physical abuse at his hands.

My father would return home, after disappearing for weeks, and if my mother chose to confront him about where he had been or mention his duty to our family, he would explode, striking her in front of my siblings and me. My older brother tried to intervene, but he was only sixteen, so his attempts at protection merely served to make him a target without protection of his own.

And through it all, we had a home, a roof over our heads, though we often lacked the essentials electricity, gas, and water. My mother struggled to keep everything as normal as possible for us, a task that with only a single paycheck was impossible. No child, at any age, should have to face these experiences. And yet, this is my story, the story of a little boy, fearful and desperate to escape the past, who still cries inside the man.

My innocence was stolen from me in multiple ways, not only at the hands of my father! And while I desperately wanted to tell my parents, I was afraid of how it would affect my dysfunctional and disturbed home, so I kept the secrets. Devastating secrets that would haunt me for the rest of my life. I wanted to lock myself away from the world and escape the pressures of my young life once and for all.

And so it began; as my father's drug abuse and the physical abuse toward my mother was revealed, little did I know that another heinous act was coming. In kindergarten, I was excited my oldest brother was going to be picking me up from school. He was one of my "superheroes," and I thought it would be so cool when he picked me up from school. I looked up to him, depended on him, and thought of him as a protector.

At first, we played video games, and it was fun! Then the unthinkable happened: a wrestling match with my oldest brother turned into something foul. Suddenly, my clothes were off and we were no longer wrestling. I was only five years old. I didn't know if this was something brothers did, or if it was WRONG! I quickly discovered how wrong it was when he came to me crying, apologizing, telling me to shower, quickly, before Elijah and Angel got home.

I knew it was wrong and so did he, but even though he apologized, he continued to do it again and again. I was only five and afraid to tell anyone. I sought the only escape I could think of and imagined happy times, blocking the physical abuse out of my mind. Needless to say, and not knowing what else to do, I began to accept what was happening to me.

I was so confused. I had so many questions, but none with answers. The depth of my fear of my brother was great; I didn't know what to do say. Today, I still remember as if it was yesterday. When I think of the abuse, I feel as though my oldest brother shattered many of my dreams. I feel as if I was sentenced to life without parole, never having a moment to catch my breath and knowing, at that time, my life was totally out of my control.

The molestation by my brother continued for some time, and when he finally stopped, it began all over again by a predator who everyone thought was a friend of the family. It was then that I began to wonder if the problem was with me. Why was I a target for abuse? Why didn't anyone realize what was happening to me? Why wouldn't anyone help me?

And these thoughts return me to the present day, understanding the fact that everyone desires a sense of security in their lives and the knowledge that they are protected. I was no different. I wanted my dad to be there for me; I wanted him to protect me. Instead, he was gone from our lives as much as he was present in them.

As an adult, I discovered my father, whom I so desperately wanted to be my champion, had a second family complete with other children. When a person doesn't show up in your life the way you want or expect them to, it can be devastating. And it takes time to realize the momentary disappointment was protection from what could have become long-term pain. Don't fall for the illusion that you've missed something you needed to survive.

Today, I have forgiven my father for falling short. In all honesty, I don't think he truly knew how to be a father. I have even forgiven my oldest brother, who, though he served time in prison for raping a young lady, has never suffered any consequences for the damage he inflicted on me, his baby brother.

The Value of My Mentors

Leadership Is Influence and Influence is Leadership: Nothing More, Nothing Less.
- **John Maxwell**, *21 Irrefutable Laws of Leadership*

And while that is true, I would like to add my own twist.

**Leadership absolutely is influence
but influence is also IMPACT.**

Leadership is influence, and leaders who use their influence over those in their sphere become mentors who guide and encourage the next generation. In doing so, they wield their influence and impact individuals with their leadership.

Impact, then, is the catalyst which engages an individual to dream again, believe again, and connect again. Impact releases a spark, a piece of magic providing a lasting effect on an individual on the road to their destiny. It allows individuals to reach beyond the surface of who they think they are supposed to be and see who they are destined to be.

The impact of leadership and mentoring allows individuals to see beyond their limitations, their economic status, their ZIP code, and their opposition. It allows individuals to realize every setback experienced in their lives is actually a setup for a comeback. It allows individuals to understand the opposition in their lives prepares them for opportunity as opportunity prepares them for their destiny.

During the transaction from mentor to mentee and from mentee to mentor, a deposit is transported from one to another, allowing both individuals to discover the importance of connection and positive relationships which, ultimately, create great leaders. And so, I ask, when are you going to start releasing your magic and discover your IMPACT? Can you kindly tell me when that day is going to come? Is it going to be tomorrow? Is it going to be next week? In a hundred years? Never? The time for leadership, the time for influence, and the time for impact is always right now! Why? Because it is what we do, it is who we are!

It's not where you come from
or where you are now
that determines your future;
it is you!

Finding Your Magic

When you decide to accomplish the amazing, it begins with your dreams. Identifying your magic can be difficult, not because it is an impossible task, but because we navigate through life with external orientation. Leadership, influence, and mentoring all act as catalysts, allowing young people to discover their magic within. These three are the very pulse which helps young people understand all they need to be great is within them. Everyone is uniquely qualified to do exactly what they have been put here to do. Release your magic and discover your impact.

I know your path may be hard; truly, I do. But I also know someday you will know exactly which road to choose. Be courageous, pick up the pieces of your life, and go forward. Impactful people cannot judge that which is within based on what they see around them.

Do you know what it is to have a fight going on inside because you did not fight on the outside? I might seem weak now, but rest assured, I am smart and I am powerful. Smart and powerful people do not hide when they have been wounded; they fight back. And one day, out of nowhere, I did just that, no longer existing as a normal individual, but speaking out and becoming a hero.

Every day offers opportunities for each of us to be a role model with our words and actions. I know now, if I had given up due to my past, I would not be where I am today. I am not all that God intends for me to be yet; I am in transition—not a caterpillar and not yet a butterfly. The thing I know for certain is I cannot turn back, I can only go forward.

You and I, we must never forget our past—remembering our mistakes helps us keep from repeating them. Instead, we must take ownership of our identity. The simple truth is you either get bitter or you get better. You can take the life dealt to you and allow it to make you a better person, or you can allow it to tear you down. The choice does not belong to fate, it belongs to you.

Your fate is not in the hands of chance, it is in your hands. Do not wait for it, but embrace it. Those who want to achieve great things must dig deep, make sharp decisions, think creatively, and hold their ground. You cannot move forward until you are willing to make a MOVE!

From My Heart

I'm trying to become comfortable in my own skin, but it is not as easy as some would have you think. It is truly a challenging process—learning what you like, what you dislike, what is comfortable for you, and what is uncomfortable.

On this journey, I have come to understand there are times which will be filled with uncertainties; but one thing is certain, regardless of what you are experiencing in the present moment, you must realize it is for that moment. We don't make life decisions based on a single moment; we make them based on our experiences and the wisdom we have acquired through those experiences.

I feel as if God is constantly encouraging me not to stop writing my story as these words continue to ring in my ears. Even so, I am still anxious and sometimes uncertain about writing this manuscript. I never thought for a single moment I would be writing a book giving others a glimpse into my life, which has been filled with so much disappointment, heartache, and uncertainty.

There are portions of my life which I continue to try and understand. Some days, I feel as if I have things under control; other days I don't. For some strange reason, I'm extremely hard on myself as relates to those things I feel are out of my control.

What type of things am I referencing? I'm so happy you asked. Things like my sexual identity, which is a daily process, my self-esteem, and the day-to-day processes of renewing my mind while coping with the realization I was molested and there is nothing I can do about it. And then I remember that to learn, I must grow and take it on one day at a time. The real issues come when

I'm debating with myself—should I really write this book, knowing by writing this manuscript, I am allowing others access to very real and vulnerable places in my life? That, in itself, is downright scary.

I have learned throughout this journey we call life, if I allow fear to set in, there is a strong possibility I may not achieve anything. You see, if I allow fear to sneak in and become rooted in the very fabric of my character and life, that fear will cause stagnation and prevent me from moving forward. Fear, then, brings me to my knees—the fear of what others might say, the anxiety of being rejected, and the dread that I might be denied access to my destiny.

It's time to faith it!
Cora Jakes Coleman

I have enough faith to realize regardless of others' perceptions, from their criticism to their conversations behind closed doors, I cannot allow them to deter me or get me off track. I am doing my best not to allow my insecurities to rob me of the blessing of God's love and favor. But even so, I need to tell you about the little boy who wanted desperately to be a man.

Still, for some strange reason, I feel so alone. I am constantly reminding myself I might seem weak now, but rest assured I am strong and God is on my side.

In God I have put my trust;
I will not be afraid.
What can man do to me?
- Psalm 56:11 (NKJV)

I have learned you should never give up on your dreams because the people who can help you are often the ones who don't help you. We must remember, man's constructs never accommodate God's ideals.

Pressure (in Focus)

In this season, the season of pressure, I got into focus and refused to lose that focus! I cannot keep making the same mistakes, repeating the past. I must make every step count the first time. I have to progress.

Whatever God has promised, it will truly come to pass. David was anointed to be king, long before he was positioned to be the king. He had to go through the process of a shepherd...praises sung to God in the lonely nights, rebukes and judgement by his brothers, giants to bring down...he had to accept the silence of obscurity so he could ultimately handle the applause. And the biggest lesson of all—never forget it is the Lord who brought him there. He had to survive the jealousy and rejection from his family and even then, there was nothing that could cancel out God's promise to him. In David's life, it came to pass! And today, the Word of God still cannot fail.

I can hear God speaking to me: *"There is a Word over your life, Danarius, and it cannot fail! Be still and know that I am God! Remember my Word, 'The battle is the Lord's! The steps of a good man are ordered by the Lord!'"*

"David moved into his destiny...YOU are not one minute early or one minute late. God is taking you through the process to arrive at His purpose in your life. While in the process, you have to give thanks! Even though you may not understand, you should simply give thanks. Appreciate the long road, because the process grooms you for greatness!"

God is and always has been faithful! Just as he is doing for me, God has been grooming you, too, for greatness. He is zeroing in on your life. God has given you the ultimate clearance! He has sent a second wind to empower you to do everything He has purposed you to do. God has given you a fresh anointing!

Sometimes you can't move forward until you recognize where you have failed. Failure teaches us where we went wrong, and helps us see that our most horrible mess provides our greatest blessing as we learn from our mistakes. For every new opportunity and assignment, we need a fresh anointing on our lives. This anointing is not something we can glean from our education. It is in the midst of a spiritual battle where you can do nothing without the anointing of God. Our greatest battles will always be fought at the door of our greatest opportunity. Be excited, because for you and me there is a door overflowing with new beginnings about to happen in our lives. Hallelujah!

Under Pressure to Find Your Purpose

When you are trying to help people, sometimes they will fight you, because between you and your dream there will always be trouble. Your dreams will cause controversy, even if they are intended to help others find their way from under the pressure of their purpose and destiny.

At some point, you must decide who you are going to be. You cannot allow someone else to make the decision for you. The very thing you are so ashamed of might just be the tool God wants to use in your future. The thing which causes you the greatest pain might be the thing which produces the greatest power in your life.

Chapter 7
Don't Miss Your Opportunity
(Give Me a Strategy)

Stories have the power to transform our perceptions of the world and ourselves. I have found the best lives are often filled with the best stories, which have provided the underlying meaning to the events in our lives. That is the power of the narrative. We all articulate our stories in some way. We tell stories about meeting important people in our lives, we use stories to explain our own idiosyncrasies, and to help give meaning to the events of our lives. Thomas King, novelist and activist, argues, "The truth about stories is, that's all we are." Sharing stories is critical in allowing individuals to connect. It is the gateway which can help people find their way, even helping them escape from a negative situation or circumstance.

More of My Story so You Can Tell Yours

You will never understand my praise until you see my past. I have learned that each of us has our own personal journeys, and those journeys intertwine with others throughout our lives. The thing is, we can't expect people who live in fear to understand our faith, making it important to always remember the opinions of our critics have no control over the outcome of our destiny.

As you begin to command your days, even in times of adversity, you will be able to say this will be the best day of your life! Neither you nor I are victims of the circumstances we live under; we are victors regardless of the circumstances we face in our lives. This step begins when you start to understand and celebrate what God has already said—then He will begin to reveal more of your destiny to you. In order to do so, you will have to know your worth, which will require an honest assessment. Once you understand your worth, you must never apologize for knowing who you are and what you need to add to improve yourself and your life.

Seizing the Opportunity

In order to seize the opportunities placed before us in life, we must organize our strategy with the right priorities.

Seize Your Opportunity

- Begin with great humility
- Defy the urge to quit
- Show up with expectations
- Take a risk
- Accept NO as a means to a better opportunity

Humility by definition is having the quality of being humble, but what does that mean, exactly? C.S. Lewis said, "Humility is not thinking less of yourself, but thinking of yourself less." Humility, then, is having enough confidence to think of others more. In addition, humility is more about what is right, and not so much about who is right. It is doing the right thing for all.

With this mindset, you can put down the urge to quit when things aren't going exactly as you planned. Since you aren't about quitting, you can keep your expectations at the forefront and not be fearful of taking risks to seize the opportunities God places in your path, remembering that "no" simply means there is something better ahead for you.

To begin, you must love the person in the mirror. This does not mean thinking only of yourself. Loving yourself, having confidence in yourself, and relying on yourself allows you to take on the world, and take advantage of the opportunities. I had to learn, as you probably have, that we must deal with the problems we face, each in our own valley, so we can take triumph in arriving on our mountaintop.

When we experience victory, that victory becomes a testimony to those around us. It comes as we develop the attitude that we will receive God's best—when we are able to do so, everything else will begin to align.

> ...pursue righteousness, godliness,
> faith, love, patience, gentleness.
> Fight the good fight of faith,
> lay hold on eternal life,
> to which you were also called
> and have confessed the good confession
> in the presence of many witnesses.
> - 1 Timothy 6:11b-12

To fight the good fight, we must develop the correct stance and position. Whenever we encounter situations in which it seems the light is not on for us, this does not mean the treasure God has in store for us is gone. We must stop believing we are defeated, many times even before we begin, so we can properly walk into our triumph, the triumph which God intends for us.

When we follow that purpose, the one God has planned for us, we will always reach the peak of our happiness. This victory is not something that just happens randomly—it is the development of the mindset that we are victorious in everything. Once we know this, when there seems to be a deficiency, we can operate at maximum efficiency with God's help!

For every trouble you and I have faced, God has set aside a blessing for us! When we begin to live out our victory even in our most difficult moments, we can see God at work as we develop a triumphant spirit, which gives us the key to living a life of continuous victories. Now is the time for you to become the master of your own destiny. No matter how difficult the situation may be, you must say, "Yes, I can!" Never forget, you are destined to live a life of victory as you yield to the true authority.

Let God Have Control

We know a bad situation will never improve by continuously talking about how difficult it is. Action must be taken, prosperity must be spoken, and then things begin to change. You must dedicate yourself to the process because when you do, there will be positive results. You cannot let the trials of your circumstances be the final verdict regarding your outcome.

The final verdict regarding your outcome comes from understanding that true authority is the justification and the right to exercise power, and it exists in the form of God, whether we choose to recognize it or not. When we allow God to be the authority in our lives, we can achieve greatness, but in turn, we must learn the cost and sacrifice it may bring. Letting God have control means submitting to His true authority.

For me, it went like this:

God, I submit myself, my purpose, my destiny, and my future over to You.

You are my foundation, my rock, my fortress, and my strength.

You are my defense.

Without You I can do nothing.

I will take no promotion unless You approve.

I will not accept friends unless You select them.

For it's in You, I live and move and have my being.

God is the ultimate authority, and He wants you to encounter Him right where you are so He can lift you up higher than you have ever been. The Bible demonstrates, time and time again, an encounter with God can make the sick well, the hurting heal, and the dysfunctional functional.

Today, there is healing—physical, emotional, spiritual, relational, and financial—in store for you. Regardless of what you are going through, be encouraged, for I am convinced this is the time for you to extend your faith. When you show God you are willing, many wonderful things begin to happen.

Even so, you should be prepared to be uncomfortable as God teaches you the lessons He has for you to make you the best person you can be—the person He wants you to be. Are you prepared for what God has for you? It means you must learn to become the full measure of who you truly are. It means when God calls you to a task, He will equip you to succeed, sending the help you need.

To receive God's victory, the way He means it for you, is gaining command of your words and actions! From my own experiences, if you allow God His true authority in your life, I can decree and declare there will be no missed opportunities. If you choose to act in your own authority or that of other influencers in your life, I can attest opportunities will pass you by. I know; I have allowed quite a few opportunities—scholarships, business ventures, promotions, and more—to pass me by due to past failures, fears, and insecurities. Even so, I need you to believe, there is no missed opportunity in God. If God said it, then that finishes it. Everything He has pronounced and decreed for your life will come to pass. You can discern those opportunities presented by God, through His Word, communication with Him (prayer), and the wise counsel of other believers (spiritual mentors).

The Opportunities with God

No matter what your current situation looks like, you must prepare yourself for what God is doing. Whatever you are facing in life, remember it is not too great for God to overcome! God will always deliver the righteous out of trouble, so in your weakest moments, put your faith in Him and watch Him work it out. Don't operate in defeat; instead, be prepared for victory, remembering any road to victory will have rough patches, but staying the course means victory will always result!

The funny thing about opportunity is you must be able to recognize it when it presents itself. But opportunity is not a person who is going to come up to you and say, "Hi, my name is opportunity, would you like to join me?" You should not only recognize it, but understand you are deserving of it when you are in the midst of an open opportunity.

We must speak positivity into our lives daily. When we speak thusly, we will begin to see it! You shouldn't miss any opportunity— I mean it! Never sell yourself short, as I have in the past, never listen to the voices of doubt in your life because if God says you can do it, then it is settled—you can do it!

Too many times, we allow our dreams, desires, and distractions to keep us from being where and doing what we should. When we do, we miss the opportunity to truly transform our lives! Don't miss your opportunities! Do you know how many people in the world are waiting, often because they don't recognize the opportunity right in front of them? It is true, but don't be dismayed: God will restore lost opportunities, lost blessings, and lost favor swiftly. You only need to ask Him.

Your Opposition Is Your Opportunity

"Your opposition is your opportunity" sounds counterintuitive, doesn't it? Maybe so, but the truth is, God doesn't put everyone through the struggles, only those he deems strong enough to handle them.

It is time to be great! When you give in and allow the negative influences in your life or from your past to rule you, you miss your opportunities. It is a big mistake too many of us make, and it is a recipe for continuing emotional pain and loss of your life's full potential.

There is a reason I am still running this race and telling you my story—I refuse to quit! The steps that changed my life and continue to do so came when I stopped being willing to settle. I always thought I was not enough, but I was and I am. I realized God never counted me out, but showed me I could love him, be myself, and be accepted by others. What an opportunity and what a fresh start for me—and it can be for you as well! Right now, believe this—God has never counted you out! Knowing that is your fresh start—one that will change your life forever.

Transition Is Very Challenging

I confess, I am in transition. I had to learn not to let my pain distract me from the purpose God has for my life. I had to discover the importance of not giving up too quickly. Once you start deleting the distractions in your life, you will be able to focus. Declare today the day of no more crying over the ones who left you. God knew they would leave, and He is using that to push you into His perfect purposes for your life. The mess you may now be experiencing is the process that will lead you to positive progress!

You can't let yourself settle for the enemy's temporary joy, because God wants to give you permanent joy. Instead you should empower yourself with the tools and support needed to address the biggest challenges standing between you and your opportunities.

Author and pastor John C. Maxwell says, "You either win or you LEARN." How true that statement is...if you succeed, wonderful...if you fall short, learn from your shortcomings, and move on to the next opportunity!

Your Message Matters

You need to know your message matters—even if you never write a book or appear on television or become a YouTube sensation, you are influencing those around you continually. So, you need to keep doing your best, even when you don't immediately see the results. And, you need to keep loving yourself, even when you drive yourself a little crazy.

This has been a difficult concept for me. If I'm honest, way too often I care way too much about all the wrong things. May this be a reminder to all of us...let's try to keep the main thing, the main thing. For each of us, it is critical that we are, with God's help, the ones in charge of our control panels.

Taking Charge and Making a Difference

Sometimes, as adults, we think we must have the perfect thing to say or do, or ask the right life-altering question at the perfect moment to move forward. But so often, what truly makes a difference is considerably difficult to perceive and understand.

One area I struggled with as a child was achieving good grades in school. I believe it had a great deal to do with the circumstances surrounding me—my family's neighborhood, my family dynamics, and my own victimization. As a youngster, growing up in Detroit, I recall dealing with low self-esteem, mental and physical abuse, and feeling as if I had no true identity. My emotional abuse was present for as long as my memory. The physical abuse began when I was five, and continued until my abuser was imprisoned for a different crime, when I was ten.

As I grew older, I couldn't fathom the idea of being successful due to the nature of my circumstances, until I was presented the opportunity to be in the company of two amazing mentors who possessed the ability to force me out of my comfort zone into what I now call a commitment zone. They saw in me something I was unable to see in myself.

From them and going forward, I have learned opposition positions you for opportunity, and opportunity prepares you for your destiny. My experiences thus far have equipped and positioned me to make a positive impact on the next generation of young men and women, who are on their way to becoming progressive leaders both locally and globally.

I was once told, "It takes courage, might, fight, and will to be exceptional. Exceptionalism is not superiority; it is simply refusing to give in to mediocrity." I hope to pass this along to you now. You must remember, you were born to be exceptional. Knowing this has inspired me to believe in and value myself, while realizing there is always conflict between the ordinary and the exceptional.

I would advise other young men and women to invest in their own life, their own journey, their choices, and the lives of others. The reality is we cannot live our lives to the fullest capacity without investing in the lives of others. Our best living does not come until we invest in someone else.

The door you have been praying for is already open before you. God is there waiting to see when you are going to have enough faith to step through the door.

In James 1:13, we are told that God tests us, but He never tempts us. Unlike Satan, who is a tempter, God is a tester. And opposition is often the test to see if we will grab the opportunity God sets before us. God tests us to strengthen us, unlike the devil, who tempts us to break us!

When God spoke His Word over your life, He built a hedge around you, so the enemy, the devil, could not see your true identity. Our misperception lies in the fact that most of the circumstances we go through today are reverberations of our past experiences. You must be on guard for the enemy, who is trying to isolate you. You are alone, but you must remember fear, isolation, and depression distort your perspective. Knowing your position in Christ Jesus gives you the power to overcome any circumstances related to your past. I refuse to go BACK.

You, like me, are an execution of God's master plan You are His creation and instrument, placed into His timetable. and designed to bring Him glory! With Him, your future will be greater than your past. Despite all you have been through, your best is coming! Instead of taking steps backward, begin to look forward toward the promises of God.

Where there is no test, there can be no testimony—no story to share. Each step in your life has a purpose. Every step is required to take you to the next level. Keep in mind, the use of the term steps implies a process—which means it is going to take a while.

What you put into yourself today and every day will result in how you react to circumstances in your tomorrow. The only way you or I will find fulfillment is by birthing what God has promised us. The same God who delivered me out of my situation can deliver you out of yours.

If You Could Only See What God Sees

All of us are born with talents and gifts, but our character must be developed, carefully cultivated, and nurtured over time. If you could only see what God sees, you would get excited about your destiny—a destiny full of promise, full of victory. Of course, there may be an obstacle in the path of your deliverance—your pride—an obstacle God has put in place so that you will humble yourself before Him. Pride is an obstacle for us all. God knows our pride can stand in the way of our destiny because in today's world, we often care more about our image than our deliverance.

Like a good book, our destiny unfolds one chapter at a time. Most of us fail to get a glimpse of who we are supposed to be because we are afraid to turn the page. I encourage you to muster your courage and be purposeful. Turn the page in your life, move to the next chapter and choose what you want written in the book of your life. Don't get stuck in an old, previous chapter, and above all, don't continue reading the same chapter repeatedly. Gather your understanding and begin the next chapter!

Our differences make us strong. Those differences are the catalysts which can launch us into the next stages of our destiny. This may mean you must give up the life you have planned and find the life waiting for you. I have learned you can have good seeds (your plans) but if you plant in bad soil, the roots and growth will be negatively affected. So, don't be troubled if you see God ending some connections in your life you deemed important, remembering God will never let you waste your good seeds in bad soil. These individuals (bad soil) can limit you with their low expectations, but God wants you, instead, to be propelled by His promises!

In turn, there are times you must thank God when things don't go the way you planned, because your present is no indication of your future! Your fate is not in the hands of chance; it is in your hands. You must not wait for it, but rather, you should embrace it. For those of us who want to achieve great things must dig deep, make sharp decisions, think creatively, and hold our ground. When you're doing your best to do the right thing—the things which change your life—don't allow anyone to tell you what you can and cannot do.

If one advances confidently in the direction of his dreams, and endeavors to live the life which he has imagined,
he will meet with a success unexpected in common hours.
Henry David Thoreau

Are You Willing to Let Go?

What you are willing to let go of will determine what you are willing to walk into and experience your destiny. Sometimes you can't move forward until you recognize your failures. Often those failures are what God uses to teach us where we went wrong and bring us our greatest blessings.

If you are following the course God has prepared, you are executing His will!

You must stop looking back and begin looking forward as you trust God to take you into your destiny. God will promote people who are willing to do what needs to be done for His will to be achieved.

God is Unconventional

You may find the greatest antidote to pride is the realization of the need for help. You also must end the negativity in your life. Now, identify the unconventional methods God is presenting in your life. Are you following His guidance, His plan for your life?

The greatest tragedy in life is not death,
but a life without a purpose.
-Myles Munroe

Following another man's purpose as your own will not provide you with happiness. But, rather, God will equip us with the necessary tenacity to overcome any obstacle trying to hinder our destiny. So, when you invest your resources on what God has given you, everything in your life will begin to change.

Where do I begin? Let me start here, Father God:
Give me the words to say unto your people,
use me in the way that you see fit,
that YOU may receive all the praise, honor, and glory.
I ask that you continue to be with this generation
as Your Word states in 1 Peter 2:9,
"But ye are a chosen generation,
a royal priesthood, a holy nation, a peculiar people;
that ye should shew forth the praises of him
who hath called you out of darkness into his marvelous light."
Lord, I thank You for allowing it to come to pass
as well as Your Word in Isaiah 55:11,
"So, shall my Word be that goeth forth out of my mouth:
it shall not return unto me void,
but it shall accomplish that which I please,
and it shall prosper in the thing whereto I sent it."
I thank you for WHO you are
and for the things you have done and are going to do.
Lord keep us ... In Your Son's Name...

Amen

Standing in the Gap

It has been nearly an impossible task for me to even begin to write this manuscript and tell my story. And with that said, I feel it is important for me express to you how crucial it is for us to stand in the gap for one another.

God has placed this tremendous burden inside of me to pray for our generation, to pray for those who are hurting and lost, with an extraordinary emphasis on youth and young adults. Professing Christians seem to be "asleep," AND NOW IS THE TIME FOR US TO AWAKE. We must step up our game, for we have a dying generation who is waiting for us. We have A DECISION to make.

Are we waiting on God to provide more, when He has said it has already been done? The enemy mocks and laughs at us while we wait at the open door—the place we only need to walk through. We have the authority to enter the presence of God boldly. It is our mindset which must change. The blood of Jesus was more than enough to open the door. Our God is more than enough. Our God is more than able. Our God is willing. Our God is faithful.

We can do this, if we will only keep the faith.

Faith cometh by hearing,
and hearing by the Word of God.
- Romans 10:17

Faith is the Word and the Word is Faith, and so when we start praying, we must take our limitations off God. God is as big as you allow Him to be. Ask and believe in God for big things. We must pursue what He has for us. Faith empowers us to obtain all God has promised us.

God's Standards of Righteousness and Your Progress

Don't allow other people's standards of righteousness to lead you into guilt and condemnation. Seek God and ask Him what He would have you to do. We are not beholden to man's standards to be righteous. Jesus already took care of our righteousness. God sees you through Jesus's sacrifice and declares you righteous. You grow in Him as you work out your own salvation with fear and trembling.

Do not allow the language of people to define you. What God says is the only definition that matters. God is in our lives to bring progress. Accepting what God has for us requires a complete life change—followed by an improvement in life's circumstances.

Never let your present circumstances halt your forward momentum. People who have the power to change do not let excuses hinder their successes. They are steadfast in their goals even when those goals are not coming to fruition. They know it does not mean those goals will not come to pass. Instead, they invest in what God has placed in them and experience the positive changes.

So, do not be intimidated by the challenges you face; God places them to make you stronger. Your troubles do not define you. And, never let failure detour you from your purpose. Don't harp on your failures, because your blessings are rooted in your willingness to get back up and try again. Starting today, step into what God has prepared for you.

You Were Created to Be a Creator

You have the power of change in you. The more you trust God with your life, the more your blessings will be revealed. This is your season to create new victories. No matter how much negativity you endure, you must never lose focus on what God has for you.

When you learn to trust God in small things, you will get a promotion to greater things. When you ask God for help, He will strengthen you in every place of weakness. Your difficult place is a great place for God to do something special. God's favor is upon you and is greater than any adversity placed before you. By beginning to understand the true nature of your problems, you can create the proper solution! It all begins with a positive mindset—the key to a positive outcome.

You can never look down on yourself, for there you will find company. Instead you must be your own self-motivator! Never let anyone stop your vision. It is okay if they don't see it your way—it is your vision, waiting to be created by you. Belief in your vision is the first step to seeing it come to pass! Removing stress from your life will allow you to dream and see your vision again. Often, God is waiting for you to disconnect certain relationships so He can open your eyes to your destiny. Don't be complacent—create the change needed to gain your victory.

You must begin to develop your vision for the future, creating a life of design and purpose. The blessings God has for you in this season are designed to unfold into something greater in the next season. God always calls us to triumph. No matter what our circumstances look like, the favor over our lives and situations is matchless. Relying on your strengths is the key to perseverance when obstacles come into your life! God's strength is made perfect in your weakness. Do you have the internal strength to persevere when opposition presents itself?

The Power of Words

No matter what the situation may seem to say, you must begin with the words of God. The winning victory begins with your words! The troubles of your life are often rooted in your words. What do you say? Take care and win the battle by wisely empowering your mouth with words of victory. Self-talk is the voice which drowns out the noisy chorus of faithless facts meant to cheat you out of your victory. What are you saying to yourself?

It is important to live by positive design, because living this way means you avoid all the trials of your errors and all the errors of your trials. If you are stuck in complacency, you will never be able to embrace your future. The road to success will always have its rough patches, but victory will be yours in the end. Regardless of your current circumstances, you must begin to speak prosperity into your life!

Transform the Way You Think and Walk into Your Destiny

You might not expect it. You might not see it coming. You might not feel ready, but God is calling you into your destiny, and it's bigger, greater, and more wonderful than you can imagine. The choice is yours today: Will you walk into your destiny?

Have you ever found yourself in a struggle, a trial, or a battle? More importantly, are you in one now? You're not alone. You don't have to face the enemy in your own strength. God is with you to save you! You don't have to fight in your own strength! The battle is not yours . . . the battle is the Lord's!

Don't let the enemy steal your joy or rob you of your peace. Even in the midst of the battle, you can fight with the assurance Jesus has already won the victory. It is your time; this is your season. This is your year to receive everything God has for you!

Think about it—you don't have to hold on to the same struggles and frustrations you had a year ago. Proverbs 4:18 assures us, *"The path of the just is as the shining light, that shineth more and more unto the perfect day."* The promise is for us, both you and me!

Whether you see it or not, the more insurmountable the obstacle... the bigger the victory. You never have to be afraid or uncertain of the outcome because the battle is not yours—the battle belongs to the Lord! Now, in case you doubt it, I'm talking about an audacious, dynamic, mountain-moving victory. The God-sized victory which no plan of man can delay and no devil in hell can stop—the kind of victory God wants you to walk in every day!

No matter what battle you might be facing today—spiritual, financial, medical, relational, emotional—be encouraged! Regardless of where you came from or what you've been through, irrespective of your situation or your surroundings, and no matter what others are saying or doing in an effort to hold you back—you have the courage and power to overcome, to break out of the dungeon of mediocrity, and live in the realm of the exceptional. The people and the circumstances around you may try to define you as ordinary, but there is one fact they do not know (a fact you may not know yourself): God has destined you to live an overcoming, exceptional life in Him. Don't waste another day living down to the low expectations others have placed on you. You are an extraordinary, exceptional child of God!

Chapter 8
You Are Never Alone
(My Obligation to You)

Even though we are children of God, when things get difficult, we all seek a hiding place, a shelter from the difficulties—but where we choose to hide makes all the difference.

> You are my hiding place and my shield;
> I hope in your Word.
> - Psalm 119:114

This is true for me, even as it is for you. There are several areas in which I struggle. Yours may be similar or completely different, but as I share, remember—I am never alone, and neither are you!

I need help with pride. I know pride is the barrier that keeps us from receiving God's strength in our weakness. Pride, like other barriers, walls, and blockages, keeps us from breaking out to live the free, holy, and exciting lives God wants us to have—more than we could ask for!

I also have difficulty with being a Christian who struggles with homosexuality. It is a battle of two worlds, forcing me to put up walls and barriers.

These barriers are limitations from the enemy placed on the treasures and riches (financial income) available to us from the Lord's storehouses. So, I pray: *Lord, please remove all the afflictions, hardships, difficulties, confusion, and burdens from me, my mother, and my whole house.*

Surely, he will save you
  from the fowler's snare
  and from the deadly pestilence.
- Psalms 91:3

And I realize through it all, God is grooming me for what He has prepared for me. I am struggling right now, and my faith has taken quite a hit this last year and a half. Even so, every time I think I am going down for the third time, the Lord pulls me back up and I know, though I sometimes fall prey to doubt, He is preparing for what he has planned for me.

Trust in the LORD with all your heart
  and lean not on your own understanding;
  in all your ways submit to him,
    and he will make your paths straight.
- Proverbs 3:5-6

Maybe the disappointments are destiny in disguise. In the Book of Judges, the Word says, *"However, his father and mother did not know that it was of the LORD, for He was seeking an occasion against the Philistines. Now at that time the Philistines were ruling over Israel."* (14:4) This is the story of Samson—the great strongman of the Bible, a judge over Israel. Though Samson failed to live up to his full potential, with his death began the deliverance of the Israelites from the Philistines. Here, early in his story, Samson's parents are taken aback when Samson chooses a Philistine wife, rather than a woman from his own people, the Israelites. Little did they know, through their disappointment, God was still working out His plan.

The same is true for you and me: even amid our disappointments, God is still at work. God has called you by name; you are His. There are no second-class citizens in the kingdom of God. True confidence is a byproduct of belonging and knowing you are never alone.

I consider that our present sufferings
are not worth comparing with the glory
that will be revealed in us.
- Romans 8:18

How Do We Know We Are Never Alone?

It is true, God is always with us. Do you believe that to be true? Why? How? As a child, I questioned that fact, and sometimes I still do today. But, I do believe it to be true. After all I have been through, I might have ended up on drugs, or in a mental intuition having lost my mind. My SITUATION should have killed me, but my SALVATION gave me LIFE! And because I am His, He promises repeatedly that He is with me. I believe Him!

Fear not, for I am with you;
be not dismayed, for I am your God;
I will strengthen you, I will help you,
I will uphold you with my righteous right hand.
- Isaiah 41:10

The Fight of My Life

As difficult as our lives may be (or have been), God has a track record of coming through for us! Of course, oftentimes in order to look forward, we must look back. We have to see God's track record in our lives to be assured of our future in Him. We must be patient and keep our faith in God's promises.

Whatever we have been through, we should learn from those experiences and bring our gained wisdom to similar situations in the present. This also means we must be careful with those we seek to exclude and count out in our lives because, as we know and have experienced, the grace of God goes BEYOND our expectations!

We must understand our true character is evident when no one else is looking. The real issues we face in life don't often come with solid, ready-made answers, but rather multiple solutions which may be unclear. We have to remember no matter the circumstances we find ourselves in, God is STILL in CONTROL!

We must position ourselves in a place of expectation, where we are ready to receive our blessings, which will allow us, in turn, to help others. Even when we face situations which go against our beliefs, we must not abandon what we know to be true about our God. Whatever God is calling us to, we must be ready, always strong and prepared for the challenges we face.

God says we are STRONG! Every tear, every struggle, and every storm has prepared us to walk in our victory. It was not meant to break us, but to BUILD us. We are God's beloved, and we are meant to be an inspiration to the world!

Our Faith in God

In times of torrential turmoil and trouble, we can most clearly gauge the sincerity of our faith in God. If we ever doubt God's willingness to completely forgive and restore us to HIM, simply remember: WE are the Prodigal Son and HE is The Father. (Luke 15)

Faith is our disciple's dedication, determination, and diligence to be ever loyal in our relationship with God, even when things are NOT going well. When you are at your weakest point, it is merely an opportunity for the glory of God to be manifested in your life. This makes it important to praise God publicly for the things you are going through privately.

I must continue to remind myself not to judge others, because you never know what is happening in someone else's life. Be careful how you evaluate people and form opinions. Always be willing to understand others' circumstances. We are all human; therefore, we should all have the ability to relate to each other. Let me be the first to say, we are not alone in this journey. It took me a while to come to the full comprehension and understanding of that truth. I finally realized how to trust God on this journey.

We must remember, God is not ordinary, but extraordinary. I am made in his image and so are you; therefore, neither of us is ordinary! Even so, we all face trials and tribulations which give us the opportunity to show our faith in God. And with that, when you find yourself uncertain about your future, know God WILL take care of you!

God does not test our faith to discover how much we really trust Him—He already knows! The test is to reveal to *us* how much we truly trust Him. We should be strong, and when it seems things are falling apart, we must maintain our character. Even when we don't know it, God is working out the details on our behalf.

Trouble is not for always. You can be sure when God forgives, he forgets. Your past cannot hold you captive. Take care of yourself so you can be there for others. Be glad for today, and leave yesterday behind.

Even when you don't understand what God is doing with His hand, trust His heart. Have faith that He is working everything out for your good. God is always faithful!

Be Careful with Whom You Share Your Dreams

Though we might like to believe everyone wishes us well, the truth is not everyone is for you! We must stop expecting loyalty from people who cannot give us even simple honesty. You must watch diligently even regarding who you ask to pray on your behalf! Jesus warned us in Matthew 10:16 with these words:

Behold, I send you forth as sheep
in the midst of wolves:
be ye therefore wise as serpents,
and harmless as doves.

We would do well to heed his words and have faith that God is about to bless you right in the face of those who PRAYED you would fail!

Even in the times that God seems to take something from your grasp, He is not always punishing you, but merely opening your hands to receive something better or to give you greater insight. The will of God will never take you where the Grace of God will not protect you...remember that! Watch and see the greatness of God's salvation.

No matter what you have done, God is willing and open to forgive you...don't let anyone tell you differently. It does not matter how far you stray, God will always be there to pick you up—believe it! Don't listen to the naysayers—we are all living by God's grace and mercy, and you must not listen to vile lies and inappropriate theology.

I am learning God is God— right in the middle of my rough mountains. Sometimes I am simply stunned by His blessings even though He is just being my loving Father and gracious provider. Remember, God will provide! No matter what is happening in your life, God will never fail you. Trust God with your life; He is "...*able to do exceeding abundantly above all that we ask or think ...* (Ephesians 3:20)."

God Is Never Without Resources

Honestly, God is never without resources. His abundant blessings allow you to build where you have been broken. Don't let where you are right now define you. God is ready to restore the blessings in our lives, but we must be willing to go through the process to gain His promises—He will not fail you!

In the beginning, there was a great void in my life. I was continually seeking validation, confirmation, and relationships from everyone except God—the only one who could have filled the emptiness I was experiencing. It was in those moments I realized the more I attempted to trust people with my life, the more I would be let down.

Everyone had their idea of how I should get through the process and save myself. One suggested I isolate myself, while another said I should admit I was not happy with myself, and yet another assured me I was not praying hard enough. All the recommendations were flawed, simply because the very things they were recommending for me were the same things they wouldn't challenge themselves to do.

The truth is we serve a God who can restore any situation and heal any circumstances. There is nothing He cannot do for you today. I can testify to that truth.

One day I was sitting in the house, praying, asking God to send me a friend I could confide in, someone I could talk to and share my challenges and shortcomings. A person with whom I could be transparent and open. I asked God to send this person into my life numerous times. Each time I asked for this person to show up, no one came.

I had to turn to God. The same God who had given me a sign that I would have the victory, but the struggle was not over—I would still have to fight. With God on our side, we, as God's people, will be victorious in every fight!

Deciding to Trust God No Matter What

And with that, I have decided to trust God no matter what. There have been times in my life when I didn't trust God, and those are the times I would always fall short or fail. Trusting God is simply believing He loves you and He has the power to help you. He wants to help you and He will help you; your job is to keep trusting Him even when you can't see the outcome. God is faithful even when you can't see Him clearly working in your life.

Christians are often called believers, but many times we would be better described as unbelieving believers. We trust our friends, the bank, the stock market, or the government more than we trust God and His Word. He promises in His Word He will never leave us. Trust Him!

In John 15:5, Jesus says that apart from Him, we can do nothing. We need to lean on Him for help with everything in our lives. Sadly, a lot of us go to church on Sunday, hear exactly what our next step should be, and then go home and try our own solutions. We usually end up desperately telling God how hard we are trying to do what we need to, all the while leaving Him out of the equation. Again, remember God is here to help us in our darkest days and our craziest decisions. God has the best plan and can turn any situation around—all we have to do is trust Him.

God wants us to put Him first in our lives, have confidence in Him, and trust Him all the time, in everything. God loves you, so TRUST Him and watch Him work on your behalf!

Feeling Alone - Your Isolation Is Not Punishment from God

So, one day I was praying again, asking God why He wasn't answering me, when I received the quickest answer I have ever received from Him. He said, "Stop asking me to send you someone, I've been here all this time. The very person you are looking for is Me."

It was in that moment, isolated, where I needed to find peace within myself, with the help of God. I had to take a long look at myself in the mirror, embrace my true self, and believe I was good enough. You need to do the same, experience the revelation—after all, you have what it takes!

God has a purpose for your life, and He has a proven record of coming through—but you cannot give up. The answer may not come when you want it, but God is always on time!

The biggest and most successful trick of the enemy is having us mistake this isolation for loneliness. It is not; in fact, this isolation is preparation! Isolation is defined as "the state of being in a place or situation separate from others: the condition of being isolated."

If you feel isolated and in a dark place, don't worry. God has not buried you, He has planted you! He is cultivating you and growing you up! Seeds root in the darkest places, destiny evolves in the darkest places, and transformation occurs in the darkest places. When God is about to renew your mind, He always takes you through a dark place. But, after the darkness, comes the light of dawn where the God of all grace will perfect you, establish you, strengthen you, and settle you!

> And the God of all grace,
> who called you to his eternal glory in Christ,
> after you have suffered a little while,
> will Himself restore you and make you
> strong, firm, and steadfast.
> - 1 Peter 5:10

Sometimes it takes that isolation to get a revelation. Treasure your moments of aloneness with God, however painful. God sets us apart for his good use—separating us unto Himself. When you are alone, you will feel isolated, as if you are watching people through a glass wall. But God has isolated you for development.

For countless years I have had well-meaning Christians tell me, "You're not praying enough" or "You're not fasting enough" or "This is not your season." For many years I listened to them, believing them wiser or thinking I was doing something wrong or I was missing something or even that God had turned away from me.

This advice left me isolated, feeling alone and disconnected, to fix my own problems. And in my isolation, I prayed, I cried, I prayed, and I cried. Every day I would get up smiling, holding my head up high, squaring my shoulders, and giving the illusion that I had it all together. In so many words, I was trying to fake it until I could make it. I was always taught if you don't feel confident, pretend you are until you gain the experience or tools necessary to make your confidence real.

It is hard to practice all these tactics in isolation. Let me be honest here: praying was not always easy, especially when I wanted to give up, but it was the solution. I didn't want to pray in the beginning, because I wanted someone, a physical person whom I could see and touch, to talk to and ease the feeling of isolation. I needed someone to talk to and be with.

And yet, in my isolation, I found myself talking to God more, cultivating a relationship, getting to the point that I could honestly tell God exactly how I felt. Honestly, through this process, I wasn't always nice to God. I can remember days when I came into my room and said sarcastically, "Thanks God, that really did hurt. You were out of line. What in the world were you thinking?" Thankfully, those moments of anger and somewhat brutal honesty allowed me to cultivate an authentic relationship with God.

And this was the ultimate goal: a full-blown relationship with God which ultimately allowed me to live a better life amid the community of believers. Join Him, share your thoughts and fears honestly with Him to help you grow. Speak with Him regularly, listening for His encouragement as He comes alongside you during the challenges.

Without laying the appropriate groundwork and training, recovery from a spiritual setback can seem impossible. But, with God, you can effectively overcome any obstacle and win any battle. You may need to be still, silence your thoughts. and meditate on the desired outcome.

The Journey to Your Purpose

The journey God has you on is His plan to grow you into your inheritance. It means you have to get your true face on and know who you really are. Once you do, you can experience incredible moments, realizing the love of God!

In doing so, you cannot allow everyone to get close to you. (Remember the well-meaning Christians doling out their not-so-good advice.) Ask God, and He will show you the positive people you should surround yourself with. Do not take his guidance lightly and chose your circle wisely.

God will always provide us with strategies to handle every situation, even the selection of friends. Even in the middle of life's craziest moments, God shows us his love and provisions.

It is important to continue calling to mind all the things God has done in the past—if God did it before, He can certainly do it again!

Along the journey, people will talk about you. Remember their words are just noise—distractions intended to take you off course. Let them have their gossip. Their version of the truth is not your truth.

Your truth, the story you wrestle with when no one is watching, is the only truth that matters. Only you know how you acted. Only you know how you behaved. And that "truth," your real "truth," will determine whether you find peace and freedom or anxiety and unrest. Every time you catch yourself doing something that makes you feel great; celebrate the moment. Do what is right and let your truth set you free!

Your self-worth will then grow as you do, and it is critical to your ultimate success, both personally and professionally. Bask in those moments when you feel you are the best version of yourself. It will build strength for you to draw on in those moments when you doubt.

Happiness does not seek; it attracts. You do not find happiness; you become happy. Happiness is a decision, not a destination; a mindset, not an amount. Your happiness is not dependent on anything, except the decision to be happy. Whatever you are seeking, remember it is seeking you as well—it is known as the Law of Attraction. You only have to stand still long enough to allow it to catch up.

I have had to learn patience in the process and constantly remind myself, it is ALL working together for your good! Sometimes we must break away from the pack to accomplish our dreams. It is in those still moments alone that the whispers of your heart will guide you.

> Faith becomes a bridge
> between where I am and where I want to go.
> - T.D. Jakes

On your journey, you are never in a fight by yourself—God is always there! Don't be afraid to fail along the way. Failure is often our best teacher; every setback exists for that purpose. It is not the obstacle that is significant, but how you choose to respond.

As you chase your dreams, come out of the gate flying. Focus on your desire to be who you were called to be. It may seem unconventional and the journey may be rough at times, but you are still here, pressing forward in your journey. Don't give up now.

God Is Going to Do Everything He Promised

The Lord is going to do everything He promised in His Word. It may be today, or tomorrow, or the next day, but in His time, you are going to see Him make a way for you out of what seems like a dead end. Though the battles have been long, you have grown stronger along the way, and you are still here. You might have thought you would never make it through your night. It may seem a wonder that you survived, but you are still here, and God is going to do everything He promised.

The God we serve is not a liar; He is a promise keeper; so, get ready for your breakthrough, because God is going to bless you. His Word says, "They that sow in tears, will one day reap in joy," so rejoice!

Wherever you are right now in this moment, I want to encourage you! Sometimes the people closest to you simply cannot see the greatness in you. Your friends, your family, your coworkers may discount you. They may leave you out. Don't take it personally, but keep being your best!

We all know there are times in life when we need to help others move forward, but if you're going to become who you were created to be, you cannot do all the carrying. If you only have people around you who need carrying, need encouragement, need prayer, need a ride, need help—your circle is out of balance. You must have those who can carry you, at times, those who can help you, encourage you, and lighten your load, as you do for them. God will supply those positive people, the community of believers. If you don't see them in your life right now, ask Him. He will provide, making good on all His promises—I know!

The purpose in life is not to win.
The purpose in life is to grow and to share.
When you come to look back on all that you have done in life, you will get more satisfaction from the pleasure you have brought into other people's lives than you will from the times that you outdid and defeated them.
- Harold S. Kushner

Chapter 9
Respect the Steps (We're Almost There)

You must respect the steps to becoming your best possible self. In doing so, you have to allow God to be your GPS/guide, protector, and sustainer, while you're on this journey.

Begin with self-examination. Have you become so familiar with your problems that you no longer see your potential? I did. At one point, I became so accustomed to them I felt as though they were a chain wrapped around me and dragging me under. That is no longer an issue because I have taken responsibility for my life and become accountable for my actions. I have chosen not to play the victim. Though I have lost some of my dreams along the way, I gained focus, self-discipline, motivation, and the desire to take part in my own life, removing myself from the captivity I had made into a shelter.

I spent a great deal of time overthinking my purpose when it was always right in front of me. I cut many corners in futile attempts to gain purpose and happiness when all I needed to do was listen to my heart and give my life to God. I'm sure I am not alone in this, but it seems I am an expert in making things more difficult than I ought.

In order to take the next step, you have to let great people flock to you without being intimidated by their greatness. Don't try to be great by yourself!

Whatever It Takes to Become Whole

You must make the decision to take the steps needed to become whole—whatever they are! Often your greatest blessings come from your most difficult trials, those in which you overcame adversity. God will use the hard times you face and turn those times into something unexpectedly great and for your good!

God has invested a great deal in you. For all the Creator has supplied in you, there is only one thing God seeks from you—the answer to this question: *"What are you doing with all I have given you?"* God expects you to work excellence out at the level given to you.

As you do so, you must remember failures are not setbacks, but rather, they are fuel. You must play the game by God's rules coupled with your own—two sets of rules. You must stop playing the game according to someone else's rules because you cannot win if you don't understand those rules. So, step out of their particular game, which is not, after all, worth playing.

For example, I bought into others' perspectives on who I was, and what I was capable of, so many times that I began to disqualify myself, doubt myself, and view myself as less than—until I learned who I was, and who God said I was destined to be.

I didn't think I was good enough for school. I didn't think I was good enough for the job I have. For so long, I didn't think I was good enough, but the reality of the story was I had to learn to let go of the labels. For so long, I thought everyone else was placing labels on me, but I was actually placing labels on myself, which stemmed from comparing myself to others, low self-esteem, and depression.

Here's a little secret: adversity, hardship, affliction, and misfortune have a funny way of helping you out...believe it or not, sometimes they even try to define our lives. Nevertheless, I had to learn how to think about and view adversity, hardship, affliction, and misfortune as just another method to hinder, paralyze, and distract me from reaching my endless potential, and you must do the same. Adversity, hardship, affliction, and misfortune seek to cripple an individual from realizing their full potential and their magic within. This is done by polluting our thoughts with negativity. And these thoughts give the odds of you actually being successful in life and not becoming a statistic.

When you change the way you think, you can change your life! These "Words of Wisdom" inspire me to rethink where I am in my life and where I am headed. You'll win if you don't quit. I've had plenty of adversity, but each incident taught me a lesson about my leadership, my strengths, and myself. No one gets by without some type of adversity, especially when you are on the journey toward your dreams!

First Lady Michelle Obama said it best: "It's important for us to understand that our experience facing and overcoming adversity is actually one of our biggest advantages. It was Dr. King who stated that the ultimate measure of a man is not where he stands in moments of comfort and convenience, but where he stands at times of challenge and controversy. Adversity often prepares ordinary people for an extraordinary destiny and it takes courage, might, fight, and will to be exceptional and to stand up to adversity."

To achieve the GREATNESS God desires in and from you...step outside the limitations those people have placed on you. Stop depending on others for the things only God can provide!

In all honesty, the reason hell has risen against you (no matter its means) is because you are about to occupy the very area hell has fought to keep you out of—the place God wants you to be! Before I could move into that place, I had to learn that at the end of the day my life will be measured not by the number of followers I have, but rather by the ONE I follow—Christ!

The very same truth is true for you. Your life will not be measured by the number of your followers, no matter how large, but by the one you choose to follow! In understanding that truth, never forget your testimony is proof the devil is a liar, and your praise is the evidence you are still alive and working toward God's goals for your life.

The enemy is never intimidated by your past. The enemy is only threatened by your future. I have learned on this earthly journey a truth which I hope you are learning now: what God has placed in you is greater than what the devil has placed in front of you. And just like Joseph, whatever is not part of our dream and God's plan for us, we are leaving behind!

Stay Safe or Step Out in Faith

The very troubles which left me feeling isolated, the trials which challenged my very existence, were the exact burdens and obstacles that ultimately cultivated me to be different from those around me. These trials were also the tests which helped me choose whether I would stay in what was safe and comfortable to me, or step out in faith and pursue my destiny.

You have the same choice today. You can play it safe, never dreaming, never realizing your true destiny, or you can step out in faith and answer the call of God on your life. Remember God's call is always for the call for His best—the call for greater influence, grander wisdom, countless favor, and more increase.

Failure is always part of life. You've had failures and so have I, but the beauty is those failures have taught me invaluable lessons about myself, my strengths, and my attributes as a leader.

Sometimes you can't move forward until you recognize your failures. God uses your failures to teach you lessons, which is why you often come out of your worst messes with your biggest blessings.

No one goes through life without failures; it is what you do after those failures that matters. Do you get up and fight another day, or do you give up and remain the same?

There are a lot of people
who will try to step on your confidence
based on their assumptions
about who they think you are.
-Michelle Obama

Who is Going to Stop You?

In all honesty, I do not need those people making assumptions about me. I don't need others to believe in me in order for me to believe in myself.

Which leads me to this truth: the question is not who is going to let me; it is whom will I allow to stop me? It is up to me. It is my move.

We must let go of the life we have planned for ourselves...in order to accept the one God has waiting for us. When I dare to be so powerful, to use my strength in the service of my vision, then it becomes less important whether I am afraid. I must be willing to go after my best life—no matter what!

The same is true for you. This is just the beginning of my story and yours. We are next in line. Jesus did not save us to compete with one another, but to complement each other!

Our circumstances do not define us. We define our circumstances. As Jesus tells us in Matthew 5:11, God blesses us when people mock, persecute, and lie about us, saying all sorts of evil things against us because we choose to follow Him. We get one shot to do that—and it is a battleground. All we have to do is get through the battle. There, we lose those things we believe to be blessings, the material things we possess, to gain our best life—the life God intends for us—the people we are about to become.

Change the Way You Think and Change Your Life

There is no truer fact than this: what lies behind us cannot compare to what God has in store for our futures. There is no battle, no possession, no obstacle, no adversary, and no devil in hell—absolutely nothing and no one can separate us from the love of God. What a promise—and one that we must keep focused on!

And I am convinced
that nothing can ever separate us
from God's love.
Neither death nor life,

neither angels nor demons,
neither our fears for today
nor our worries about tomorrow
—not even the powers of hell
can separate us from God's love.
- Romans 8:38

Why would God choose someone from the northwest side of Detroit, who was abused, used, rejected, and molested? Why select someone who, as a child, was labeled retarded? Why pick someone who had a speech impediment? Then I sit and thank God for isolating me from the world around me, raising me to stand against injustice, and be a proponent for equality.

Some of the things that happened to me weren't about me at all, at least not in the moment. Instead, the incidents were positioning me where I could ultimately be effective in serving others, motivating, mentoring, inspiring, and helping others to heal, as I did.

Remember, you have the power of choice. While you cannot control everything that happens to you, you can choose to control your response. You can choose not to be reactive, remembering that perspective makes all the difference. And you are now viewing your life from God's perspective!

Your unresolved problems will drive you away from people and alienate you from God. Those issues will put you on an island by yourself. Unresolved problems will disconnect you from those around you until you find yourself in an isolated situation where you will be intimidated and insecure.

On the other hand, your God-given abilities, passions, and experiences are all components which make up your character. By engaging them and resolving your problems, you can avoid a lot of unnecessary detours and discover the assignment God has fashioned just for you, even when you have NO IDEA the IMPACT you are making.

When you are doing your best, doing the right things, the ones that can change your life—don't let anyone stop you! Don't let people use you, disrespect you, or try to fool you. Don't be troubled if you see God ending some of the connections in your life, knowing that He will never let you waste your "good seed in bad soil." (Mark 4:8) Trust your gut regarding those who enter your life, and know when to walk away.

Your fate is not in the hands of chance, it is in your hands as God plans it. You should not wait for it; you should reach for it. Those who seek great achievements in life must dig deep, make sharp decisions, think creatively, and hold their ground because the most worthwhile battle will be fought at the door of our greatest opportunity.

Your personal focus is required to experience God's divine provision. Like me, you are called to be a leader—a person who has found his calling—the call so natural and authentic that when you are doing it, you are simply being you. Leadership is the capacity to influence others through inspiration, generated by passion, motivated by vision, brought by conviction, and produced by purpose.

Don't Judge When You Only Have Half the Story...

I don't know about you, but I don't want one friend that God doesn't want me to have. God places people in our paths—and us in theirs—so we might be a blessing to one another. But we don't know everyone's story, and we have to remember how powerful our voice is in encouraging others.

With that voice, we can change the narrative of our own lives and the lives of others. In my own narrative, my most embarrassing moment which brought me my greatest shame became the most beautiful transformation in my life. The situation was not fair, but God is fair. If you will let go of the pain and move forward, God has promised to bless you. As long as you hold on to the old pain, it will keep you from the new thing God wants to do in your life.

Holding on to the old pain often results in depression caused by thinking too much about the wrongs you have experienced. Most people cannot free themselves from the wrongs, even though the wrongs can be replaced by the rights and freedoms God wants to bring into your life.

You never really understand a person until you consider life from his or her point of view. Their greatest moment is often hidden in the mess of their lives. Remember, Jacob only had a ladder. Joseph only had a robe. Moses only had a rod. Joshua only had a shout. Gideon only had a sword. David only had a stone. Elijah only had a mantle. But we have something much greater to complete our story—we have the name of Jesus.

We must remember there is power in the name of Jesus, there is healing in the name of Jesus, and there is deliverance in the name of Jesus! You see, all the people I mentioned had some type of artifact or tool. But we have the best weapon in our arsenal, which is the name of Jesus.

We have a great example in Dr. Cindy Trimm's *Commanding Your Morning Daily Devotional*, where she stated, "I started to pray and to release in the atmosphere the following prayer: 'I declare in the name of Jesus that I am a pioneer of new territories. I walk in favor with God and man, and I will possess all the land God has given me. There will be no holdups, no holdouts, no setbacks, or delays. I will not look back to return to the old. Father, cause me to ascend into new realms of power and authority and access new dimensions of divine revelation. Breathe new life into every dormant dream. In the name of Jesus, Amen.'"

The Power of Closing a Door

It sounds counterintuitive, but there is great power when you learn to close a door, even in those times that require force. It is not about your excellence as a fighter, but more about the cause for which you are fighting.

Have you ever wondered if maybe you are stronger than you imagine? I have come to the conclusion, perhaps I am stronger than I think... having the capability of overcoming despite my shortcomings. I have the ability to make an impact, to have influence, and to redefine life as I see it. Perhaps this is true for you as well—there is more to you than meets the eye.

Sometimes the simplest questions can be the most complex ones. Asking yourself what you are doing and why, for example, has profound implications. Think about it—if your goal is breaking new ground, then taking territory back from someone who took it from you is a challenge.

> When a person doesn't show up in your life
> the way you want/expect them to
> it can be disappointing.
> It takes time to realize that
> the momentary disappointment
> was actually protection from
> what could have become long-term pain.
> Don't fall for the illusion
> that you've missed out on anything
> you needed to survive.
> Life isn't equal,
> but God's grace levels the playing field.
> -Sarah Jakes Roberts

There are people in your life, like those in mine, who have disappointed you, hurt you, and failed you. To live your life fully, you must discover what connected you to them and whether maintaining that connection is healthy for you. Nothing exposes people's character more than the way they treat others. Don't let those people suck your oxygen.

If the connection with them is bad for you, you may find you must close that door. Sometimes you have to be willing to leap, climb, or step over obstacles in your way in order to become your best self.

I know you possess perseverance and have a high level of determination. You have the ability to stay focused and work hard to accomplish your dreams. You've seen doors open along the way, but you've also seen doors close. Don't let that discourage you. Look for another opportunity. You have great qualities. Often, situations don't resolve as quickly as we would like, but I truly believe there are many more doors yet to open for you. It just may take a little more walking to get through those doors.

Now that I have put the answer key in front of you, you have the ability to put those obstacles in your life behind you. You cannot allow what happened to you in the past to be your headline in the future.

I refuse to allow what happened to me at age five become the headline of my story at age thirty. I will not allow my past life to write my future headline! God is setting the stage for me as He is for you. The very people who laughed at me, talked about me, and discredited me are the same people who will be trying to befriend me when God is finished molding my life into the success He has planned for me.

As you move forward and transform your life, not everyone will understand your desire to do so. That's okay. It isn't their journey to understand, it is yours! You don't even have to know where you're going; you only need to distance yourself from what you used to be.

Radical Faith Requires Action

Your life transformation will require radical faith—something bigger than you! There is a giant with your name on him standing in your way, and he will only come down when you tap into your spiritual inheritance. And remember, you have a history of overcoming! God will be by your side, just like he was for David, for

Joseph, and for other great heroes of faith. You are destined for greatness—don't ever lose heart, for God is with you.

I'm praying you won't let those who left you or failed you have power over you and limit you. These changes you are making are not about change for the sake of change, but about making progress.

With every opportunity I am given, I work to pay it forward and encourage others to pursue their dreams and goals. If you have a dream, go for it! Never allow anyone to tell you that you're inadequate. It is your INADEQUACY that QUALIFIES you!

It doesn't matter who came before you, who jumps in your way, or who works to hinder your moment to shine; their efforts to do what you were created to do will only bring more attention to you. Today, let your light shine!

And remember this: there is something very liberating about getting knocked down. Maybe it is the fact you always find the strength to pull yourself together and keep pushing forward.

What tough little creatures we humans are—our souls, hearts, and energy are tested constantly, but we always prevail. When bad energy forces its way in, we find a way out. What comes to you is what you allow, so here's to more challenges and better experiences.

I'm so excited about my destiny that I don't have time to consider my history. You should feel the same—everything you experience is only preparation for your destiny. Personal victories, yours and mine, should become generational blessings.

You Are Where God Wants You

No matter what your current circumstances are, you are exactly where God wants you. God will not move you into another situation until you learn how to love Him in your current situation.

This is why the STEPS are so important! The STEPS are strategies designed to bring tenacity and elevation with promise and supportability. The STEPS are:

S - Strategies
T - Tenacity
E - Elevation
P - Promise
S - Supportability

Taking these STEPS teaches us to accept the circumstances and move forward into God's best for us. Knowing that, we must:

1. Always respect the STEPS.
2. Never skip a STEP.
3. Know there is always another level to be reached.
4. Choose to continue the upward climb or back down.
5. Remember God is supporting you along the way.
6. Get back up and try again if you fall down.
7. Remember rule #1.

Take the STEPS toward your dreams. You will be amazed where perseverance will take you. Keep going. I am rooting for you! Every hardship teaches you not to skip the steps to recover. Even after a great fall, you can learn to respect the STEPS that will take you higher.

The steps of the righteous man are ordered by the Lord.
Psalms 37:23

A Declaration in Light of Taking the STEPS

I come into agreement with the Supreme Court of Heaven: "We are seated in heavenly places with Christ Jesus; therefore, I war from this plain and realm."

I declare accordance with Psalm 139:14 that we are fearfully and wonderfully made.

I decree and declare that we know who we are, why we are here, and where we are going!

I decree and declare that we advance to new levels, new

dimensions, new realms, and new territory.

I declare that we shatter glass ceilings, smash spiritual bars and iron membranes.

I declare that a breakthrough atmosphere be established.

I recalibrate the spiritual climate and decree every bit of lukewarm energy must be replaced with the fire and the zeal of God.

I take authority over demonic and satanic atmospheres and climates created by cultic activity, destiny-altering images, incantations, ill-spoken words, witchcraft, hostile environments, fear, terrorism, racial discrimination, ethnic hatred, and violence.

In the name of Jesus, I command the spiritual climate to shift, along with the economic climate, the social climate, the cultural climate, the educational climate, the political climate, and the ecclesiastical climate.

I command the atmosphere be filled with the Glory of God praying, "Father fill the atmosphere, fill the environment with Your Glory."

I alter this environment and **declare** it is now suitable for my ministry to thrive, my relationships to thrive, my children to thrive, my loved ones to thrive, my business to thrive, my ideas to thrive, my nation to thrive, my government to thrive, and my economy to thrive. I establish a supernatural environment for miracles to occur.

I declare war in the name of Jesus!

Stepping into the Next Level

Now you are ready to step into the next level, where you have to be steadfast and unmovable. You must balance those who need you as well as those who feed you. Your joy cannot be full when your life is out of balance.

When it comes to being an effective leader,
it is important to get beyond the people that "need" you
and find people that "feed" you.
Everyone needs nourishment,

but sometimes we get too entrenched in our comfort zones
to get the enrichment necessary
to be the leaders we were chosen to be.
-Bishop T.D. Jakes

All of those who left you could not stay, and those who stayed couldn't leave. Stop trying to be grounded in people who are on their way out of your life. This is your year, your DESTINY, and you can't waste your time dealing with someone who is not grounded. Your heart is too rich to plant it in poor soil! (1 Corinthians 15:58) Hold yourself to a higher standard than others hold you to, and you will outperform your greatest competitor and succeed against all odds!

What you have been through and where you are from is not as important as the One who made you. He takes the foolish things of the world and amazes the wise. God can save and use anyone for His purpose, which brings me to my greatest challenge. It is easy for me to encourage others because I see greatness in them. It is much more difficult for me to see greatness in myself. Even so, my God specializes in making the underdog an overcomer, and He can do that for you and me!

"I come in agreement with Dr. Cindy Trimm as I pray the following prayer. "

This is your year; this is my year; this is the year of advancement—of overcoming and achieving more than you thought you could. To reap a harvest in your life, you must discover what it means to go deeper in your faith. When you are grounded in Christ, you can experience God's best. Laying that foundation is a precursor to receiving God's blessing and favor!

Chapter 10
Higher Ground
(It's Me)

I have learned the only limitations I possess are the limitations I have placed upon myself. I do not just want to work an eight-to-five job—I want to elicit change, I want to inspire people to chase their dreams, and most importantly, I want to help people be comfortable in their own skin.

I have learned in order to reap a harvest in life, you and I must discover what it means to go deeper in our faith. When we are grounded in Christ, we can experience God's best. Laying that foundation of faith is a precursor to God's blessing and favor.

Publishing This Book

My greatest challenge is I find it easy to encourage others and see the greatness in them, while it is difficult for me to see greatness in myself. I believe publishing this book will help me accomplish my goals of encouraging others and eliciting positive change in the world.

I believe publishing a book is more than just arranging the words together on a page. It is about accomplishing a dream, fulfilling a lifelong desire, and proclaiming my story to the world. When I stopped caring about others' opinions of me, I understood true freedom. As I began to consider writing this book, I came to an understanding: God was calling me and challenging me to stretch myself beyond my limitations, beyond my experiences, and taking me outside of my comfort zone so I would experience the true meaning of unlimited resources.

Tapping into my capabilities allowed me to understand God didn't give me limited resources, but He gives me unlimited resources! I had to say yes to the stretch, or I would have never known or understood the concept of my access to God's unlimited resources. I discovered there are limitations with my God...and because I serve an all-powerful God with no limitations, there are no limitations within me. Instead, there is untapped potential, as well as unlimited resources and endless possibilities.

Reaching Higher Ground

The greatest battles you will ever engage in will not be encounters with other people, but the battle within yourself. It is the battle within your mind for your mind. Your mind is the place God's promises are planted, the garden where the fruit of your labor grows. You must fight to bring every thought in your mind into captivity for Christ. You must gain control of your thoughts before they manipulate and destroy you.

> For the weapons of our warfare
> *are* not carnal
> but mighty in God for pulling down strongholds,
> casting down arguments
> and every high thing that exalts itself
> against the knowledge of God,
> bringing every thought into captivity
> to the obedience of Christ,
> and being ready to punish all disobedience
> when your obedience is fulfilled.
> -2 Corinthians 10: 4-6

Even now, your obedience may not yet be fulfilled and you may not be exactly where you would like to be, but you can still be thankful for the progress you are making. A strong man knows how to keep his life in order. Even with tears in his eyes, he can still say

"'I'm fine" with a smile. I did it for years until I realized God was working on me to make me transparent and to help me reach His higher ground.

Like mine, your opportunity for increase always begins with change. Yet change is not easy. We must realize that God often does His most significant work while we are in transition—out of our element, uncomfortable and vulnerable. By allowing myself to be vulnerable and permitting God to work in my life, today I can say:

"Hello, I'm Danarius,
not to be mistaken for my past self,
though I know we may look alike.
One might say we are twins.
I would argue if you look a little bit deeper,
you'll see the person you're looking for
is no longer here."

Don't Write Me Off!

So, I must ask that you not write me off, because my God doesn't write anyone off! God never says, "Oh, He's too bad!" or "No, she is not good enough!" No matter how lost or how broken things may be in your life, God will never write you off! Remember, the attacks on your life have much more to do with who you might be in the future than who you are today or have been in the past. The enemy fears you are becoming who God has made you to be. The struggles you face are meant to stop you, but regardless of the situation you are facing right now, whether it is a raging storm or a tide of uncertainty, you can find safety in the secret place of the Most High!

I will lie down and sleep in peace,
for You alone,
O Lord,
make me dwell in safety.

- Psalm 4:8

Grace for Favor

This is my season of grace for favor. This is my season to reap what I have sown. And it can be yours as well. Don't leave this earth having let everyone use you but GOD. Faith is following instructions even when they don't seem to make sense.

"For My thoughts *are* not your thoughts,
Nor *are* your ways My ways," says the LORD.
"For *as* the heavens are higher than the earth,
So are My ways higher than your ways,
And My thoughts than your thoughts.
- Isaiah 55:8-9

God wants you to know, just as He is teaching me, you are smart, you are intelligent, you are talented, you are astonishing— made in the image of God. How many times does He have to remind you? It's time for you to accept who you are and understand that He is working out His plan in your life—not your plan!

You are a walking, talking, living, breathing testament of the unstoppable, uncontainable, barrier-breaking nature of God Himself. As such, you are always only one faith-filled decision away from change, prosperity, and success. May God inspire and empower you to make the right decisions today!

As a faithful follower of God, you can initiate the closing of a painful chapter of your life and the opening of doors of opportunity. You can make a comeback from every setback! If you are prepared, and you know what it takes, making the decision is never a risk.

You can determine the path. There is always a way. Don't be concerned about what you will lose, but hold on to your integrity, and make the choice to follow God.

You know, for my whole life everyone has wanted me to be normal, so they can have company in their mediocrity. But that is not God's plan, nor is it mine. It is actually pretty simple: mediocrity is not an option. I don't want to be mediocre, and neither should you.

Your mouth should speak life even when everything around you appears dead or dying. There is nothing—no sin, no situation, no devil in hell—that can separate you from the love of God (Romans 8:38-39). So, stop drowning yourself so that others can swim. Don't give away to anyone more than you are capable of giving yourself. In almost every instance, if it doesn't feel right, it is wrong. Now is the time for you to have more authentic conversations with your real self, make the change and accept God's grace for favor.

God Is in Control

Learn to say this to yourself whenever trouble is on the horizon: God is in control. This is the key to rising above everything and everyone getting between you and your dreams. It is the key to overcoming every barrier in your life! We must remember once we've put it all in His hands, it should stay there. Let God complete the work in you!

Your voice can truly make a difference, once you have come to the realization that God is in control and is able to help you conquer the enemies and obstacles you face. Life is truly a generational relay, with each succeeding generation responsible for passing the baton safely to the next with all the refined knowledge, experience, and wisdom intact.

When it comes to fixing our biggest problems, there are no shortcuts. We should embrace forgiveness, not only for ourselves, but for others. We should communicate to those around us how much they truly matter.

Remember, our past is not what defines us, but instead it prepares us for the future. I have learned the only limitations I have now are the limitations I place upon myself. I must continually remind myself I am here to fight, to conquer, to prosper, to rise, and to thrive.

It's Time to Think Like a Champion...

Thinking like a champion begins here—you can make a mistake, and not be a mistake. Beware of allowing people to confine you to what they see you as or who they believe you to be—they cannot see IN you. God is the only one who can do that, and He is in control!

And one more thing: God is comfortable with our discomfort, even when we are not. For the next seven years, I plan to experience nothing but endless miracles.

In this stage of my life all I want is results, real, positive results. I want to experience results in my prayer life, results in my personal life, results in my relationships, results in my emotions, results in my health, and results in my career. Real results with real scars from the success of real battles. It is all a matter of learning how to take inventory while taking territory.

I can testify from my own experience and the testimonies of others, pressure prepares you for purpose. As I take a moment to reflect on my past, tears begin to fill my eyes as I think about how I survived the things I had to endure. Instantly, in my mind, I can hear His voice: pressure doesn't have to break you; instead, pressure can actually strengthen and prepare you for greater accomplishments in the future.

I have said this before, and it bears repeating: the greater your struggle, the greater your blessings. In truth, the depth of your past is a direct indication of the height of your future.

Isn't it amazing what can happen even when people label you, doubt you, dismiss you, or discourage you while never considering God's incredible plan for your life as you honor Him? God doesn't put the people you want in your life; He puts the people you need to push you to the next level—which might include haters, motivators, and gladiators, just to name a few.

When you discover the unique creation you are in God, you won't spend your life trying to copy everyone else. I want to encourage you today to start living life without regret and with no backward glances. Make up your mind to follow after God in pursuit of all He has for you. When you do, nothing will be able to stop you, not even your past!

Teaching People How to Treat You

I often hear advice stating the importance of teaching people how to treat you. What does this really mean? What does it actually look like? To teach people how to treat you, you do not begin with them, but with yourself.

At some point, you must learn to stop apologizing for being yourself. It is a hard lesson, or at least it was for me. Now, I have high expectations for myself, and I refuse to apologize for having those high standards. Mediocrity is not an option for me! It is plain and simple: I just don't want to be mediocre. Do you? Of course not, but how do you begin to reach those high expectations, so others can see you as you truly are?

To embrace the new you, you must release the old you. Your past is too heavy to drag into your future. Let it go! Say goodbye! Pronounce the benediction over your past! I decree the old things are passed away for you; behold, all things become new!

> Therefore, if any man be in Christ,
> he is a new creature:
> old things are passed away;
> behold, all things become new.
> - 2 Corinthians 5:17

Remind yourself of just how great you are, and don't listen to those who would make you commonplace—you are far from common. Once you believe in the new you, people will treat you differently.

Your destiny is not based on what is in front of you at this moment. Your destiny is based on who is inside of you! You belong to God, you are His unique creation, destined for greatness.

> But you belong to God, my dear children.
> You have already won a victory over those people
> because the Spirit who lives in you
> is greater than the spirit who lives in the world.
> - I John 4:4

My best days are still in front of me, and so are yours! Everything will be all right. God has declared it. Now is the time for me, now is the time for you, and today is our time to rise, shine, and live triumphantly.

Let God Lead

I have learned when you speak God's words over yourself and allow God to lead you, you let Him take what was meant for evil and use it for good in your life.

> As for you,
> you meant evil against me,
> but God meant it for good,
> to bring it about that many people should be kept alive,
> as they are today.
> - Genesis 50:20

Though there may be those in your life who have tried to harm you and those who spoke evil against you, as well as those who continue to do so, God is always with you, always ready to lead you. Sometimes it is hard to see where God is leading, just as it is often difficult to understand what God is teaching. But, regardless,

God is with you. Don't let that liar, the devil, deceive you and cause you to believe anything else! We are in a battle and we must all be on the same side, otherwise, we will not be able to defeat the enemy and progress forward.

Jesus is our King, and those who lead His army forward in victory must have the knowledge to defeat the enemy and save the lives of those following in their footsteps. A great leader seeks the trust of those he or she leads and takes time to learn and understand the battle.

The Bible teaches us to trust no man, so followers must pray to God for wisdom and guidance. As a leader, you should not trust yourself, but trust in God to show you the way!

God's Word tells us to pray for our leaders even before we pray for ourselves. If we are instructed to pray for the leaders of our country, how much more should we pray for the leaders who will guide us to God?

Your Higher Purpose

If we can't serve God in the small objectives, why would He give us a higher purpose? We are not serving for position. We must be serving for a purpose. If you serve God's purposes, He will put you in a higher position. We must not try to serve a purpose that is not ours.

I cannot fulfill your purpose. You cannot fulfill my purpose. Get into your position and serve your purpose. God has equipped you to fill your unique position and purpose. We are powerful when we serve our exclusive purpose!

Seek to serve the purpose God has given you. Never once did David seek to be the King of Israel, but God gave him that purpose and position. Often, he felt he was not worthy, and many times he failed, but even his weaknesses could not stop God's plan.

The same is true for you: your weaknesses cannot stop God's power or His plan; they simply create the capacity for His mighty power to work in your life. Never forget opposition does not preclude the presence of God, but provides an opportunity to prove the presence of God in your life.

We have been taught, incorrectly, that we must come to God in the right way or we shouldn't come at all. It is simply not true, and it makes it difficult for us to come to God and share how we truly feel. We are fearful of crying out to God.

As children, we were told by our parents if we didn't stop whining and crying, they would give us something to really cry about. God is not like that. He wants us to cry out to Him with our fears, our sadness, even our anger, so He can meet our needs and make us stronger and more like Him.

It is difficult to fight what is in your mind, which is often territory held by the enemy. These strongholds in our minds keep us from crying out to God even when our heart is overwhelmed by prayer, and our minds fail to keep up with our spirit.

I don't fight my mind in my mind. I can't win on that level. I have to get higher, gain altitude, and bring the battle to an elevated level. I pray aloud, yes, right out loud! I fight my mind with my mouth.

You can do it too! Sometimes it is in the darkest caves of your life that God brings it all together and sends you what you need because it is in those darkest moments that you truly get real with God.

I can tell you without any doubt my greatest storms in life were God's blessings in disguise. When I was blinded by my doubt, fear, anger, and pride, instead of running toward God in the storm, I chose to run in the other direction.

Only with the help of my friend, Claudia, who has been there and believed in me, was I able to turn to God and by His grace stand stronger each day. She is my angel with no wings. With her in my life, I am blessed more than one man should be.

God is always there; all I have to do is walk in faith and trust Him. God's love fills me even as I long for the love of a wife and children. And yet for now, God's love sustains me, giving me joy and hope as I step forward in His love.

You can take that step forward, toward God, not allowing the enemies' strongholds to imprison you. ACCEPT each moment you face in its circumstances, seeking to understand your reaction to that moment. Face the fact of how you handled it, forgiving yourself and the others involved. Accept everyone around you and everything that unfolds before your eyes as part of God's plan for your life. One day you will say, "I could have dealt with that a little differently, I'm sorry," or, "I am so glad it happened that way, thank you."

Don't let your attitude be a byproduct of your circumstances. If you do your emotions will always be out of control. If instead, your attitude is not a result of your circumstances but rather a result of the character of God residing within you, you will be amazed at what you can accomplish.

This is your time. This is your moment. God has equipped you, empowered you, and anointed you. No weapon formed against you can prosper. Pay no mind to the people trying to discourage you. God didn't put the promise in them; He put the promise in you.

God will not allow any person to keep you from your destiny,
though they may be bigger, stronger, or more powerful.
God knows how to shift circumstances
and get you where you are supposed to be
– right in the center of His plan for your life.
I know it to be true,
He did for me and
He will do it for you.

Ransomed

With that being said, I want to take this moment to remind you that you have been ransomed! I agree with Dr. Cindy Trimm, Founder and CEO of Cindy Trimm Ministries International. We are living in a prophetic hour, and according to the prophetic book of

Jeremiah, in chapter 31, verses 11-14, "the Lord hath redeemed Jacob and *ransomed* him from the hand of him stronger than he. Therefore, they shall come and sing in the height of Zion and shall flow together to the goodness of the Lord, and they shall not sorrow anymore."

The Prophet Jeremiah use the word *ransomed*, and associated it with deliverance, blessing, breakthrough, and celebration. Ransom, by definition, is to extricate from the undesirable state. Synonyms for ransomed include delivered, discharged, emancipated, loose, redeemed, released, rescued, saved, uncaged, unchained, and unfettered.

Ransomed—A place in God, with God, where you see yourself liberated, in a new spiritual location, with a better economic situation, as well as an empowered emotional persuasion, and an awesome mental revelation.

Ransomed—to break free, to live free, to be debt-free, drama-free, disease-free, depression-free.

I decree and declare over your life that even as you have been *ransomed,* you will no longer experience any sadness, sickness, and sorrow.

Through the blood of Jesus Christ, the Supreme Court of Heaven has announced tonight that you have been *ransomed.* Your children have been ransomed, your finances have been ransomed, your marriage has been ransomed. And now, if I can get you to shout tonight:

"I've been ransomed!"

EPILOGUE

"For I know the plans and thoughts that I have for you,' says the LORD, plans for peace and well-being and not for disaster to give you a future and a hope."
-JEREMIAH 29:11 AMP

I applaud the fierce boldness of Dr. Hemphill's deeply personal and gripping account of his journey through the odious "hell" of multi-faceted childhood abuse and its insidious consequences. His passionate evisceration of the weighty shroud of unspeakable pain, rejection, shame, stolen identity and frayed relationships that plagued his existence and incarcerated his destiny is a glaring testament to his fortitude. His commitment to survive by a million stitches of truth rather than die from the consequences of numerous lies and many complex, undeserved wounds is his compass through life's troubled waters.

Dr. Hemphill's personal tapestry of survival and salvation is an important and practical weapon in the arsenal of freedom for those who struggle through the maze of stolen innocence and lost identity. Thus, the reader must not fall prey to the tendency to embrace his story as simply a personal pathway to survival, but rather as an invitation to strategically navigate the minefields that are characteristic of people who live with the scars inflicted by their abusers, family and others. The proverbial, "drumbeat" of his account is clear; everyone can experience freedom by embracing a living faith that rejects limitations, pursues purpose, understands processes and practices persistence.

Dr. Hemphill does not assert that his journey has ended, nor is his prescription a panacea for the profound pain and bewilderment that accompanies the challenge of grasping the hard facts of his experience with abuse, betrayal and identity theft. This is especially true where his process is acerbated by the identification of those who are viewed, by their silence and omissions, as enablers. His courageous election to engage principles that are battle-tested lifelines is the hallmark of his roving success. Principles such as his dynamic faith, self-acceptance, forgiveness, unconditional love and an unyielding marriage to a resilient lifestyle are planks embedded in the steep climb that gives birth to sustainable victory.

His story reminds me of the symbolism I embrace when reflecting on the occasion of my scaling the pathway of the Great Wall of China. The climb was steep, long and winding, yet numerous people embarked on the journey, propelled by their individual pace and their separate desire to ponder the dynamics of the journey. Everyone was aware of the many centuries of conflict and war that necessitated the Wall and of the promise of incredible air, and of a one of a kind view at the top. The journey and the arrival to the top did not disappoint. The view in the air can only be experienced by those who embrace the process. Like the struggles of Dr. Hemphill and a multitude of others, the places of "air" and "great views/visions" reside at the end of a process of faith, struggle and appreciation of the "moments along the way".

Flanking Dr. Hemphill's storied purpose and a winding process is his evangelical fervor aimed at identifying and empowering those who endure similar plights with his message of hope, encouragement and penetrating answers to incomprehensible darkness and pain. It is fitting that our Father of glory would choose his servant to champion the cause and the recovery of those who have been marginalized by trauma. Like a master teacher, drenched in the sweat of his own "process", Dr. Hemphill heralds the call, beckons the on-lookers and gathers the broken to the wellspring of new life. May all who are empowered by his message realize that the climb starts anew and chose to embrace their journey, ascending to new heights in life and in vision.

—Honorable Donald Coleman, Pastor &
District Court Judge

ACKNOWLEDGMENTS

Wrongfully Convicted is not only my story, but it is my victory, my success, and the venue I needed for my wounds to be fully healed—from the inside out. I'm opening my heart and sharing my life, so the next time you stumble you won't sit and doubt yourself, but realize you can get back up and keep fighting.

The only reason I have the capacity to say something of this magnitude is because of the grace of God. Clearly, without God, none of this would have been possible. I am forever grateful and humbled by His presence in my life.

No matter how I feel, good or bad, happy or sad, God is still good and worthy to be praised! With the release of *Wrongfully Convicted,* I hope to relay to my readers all the struggles, strategies, and the triumphant victories taking place within me. As I expose my inner self, I hope others who have gone through similar experiences realize they, too, can be healed of the self-inflicted shame, depression, and baggage attached to molestation and abuse.

To my family and friends: You mean the world to me. Thank you for being part of my journey as I navigated through the highs and lows. You have been there every step of the way to encourage me, to challenge me, and to dare me to go deeper and to push myself to greater heights.

To my spiritual leaders: I cannot express the words to characterize what I am feeling right now, but I say, with tears in my eyes, I am forever grateful for both of you. You have been a part of my journey since day one. If I needed a shoulder to cry on, someone to depend on, or someone to bring me back into focus—you have done an outstanding job. From you both, I have learned being an effective leader means going beyond the people who "need" you to find people who "feed" you. Everyone needs nourishment, but sometimes we get entrenched in our comfort zones and fail to get the enrichment necessary to be the leaders we were chosen to be. Thanks to both of you for helping cultivate the man I am today.

To my mentors: The question remains, "How far can one go with the gifts God has bestowed on them?" Thanks to you, I now see there is no place I cannot go, there is no territory I cannot take, and there is no wall I cannot break. Because of you, I have a clearer path and the capacity to soar even higher.

To my social media network, which includes followers and friends: You are outstanding. Continue to do great things, because you never know the impact you are making. *Wrongfully Convicted* is not just another book, but a testament and a revelation of God amid our struggles. The book teaches you to be a dreamer like Joseph, who in spite of the difficulties and roadblocks placed on his life, continued to trust God, believing *You Will Win if You Don't Quit*!

About the Author

Danarius Monroe Hemphill, also known as "Dr. D", has traversed the halls of academia and earned five degrees including:

- Doctor of Education in Educational Leadership
- Master of Arts – Social Justice (Public Policy)
- Master of Education
- Specialist in Education Ed.S.
- Bachelor of Science from Alabama State University

He is one of the newest and freshest emerging voices of our generation. He is a leader, educator, speaker, activist, and generation-changer who truly understands the importance of leaving a positive impact and legacy for future generations of progressive leaders in Metropolitan Detroit (his community), the United States, and abroad.

Dr. Hemphill, is the founder of Individuals Making Progressive Achievements and Continuous Transformation (I.M.P.A.C.T.) Leadership Academy, a non-profit mentoring program. He believes "it is imperative that individuals have the ability to be willing to go the distance despite their limitations, obstacles, opposition, and restrictions," with the understanding "greatness always starts with an individual, and the individual is YOU."

Dr. D is committed to making a serious, long-term investment in our next generation of progressive leaders—right now! He is an honest speaker, a candid activist, and an agent of change, who truly understands the importance bringing about positive change.

Dr. D is one of the 100 Black Enterprise Modern Men of Distinction, an honor recognizing men who epitomize the BEMM tagline "Extraordinary is our Normal" in their day-to-day lives by presenting authentic examples of the typical black man rarely seen in mainstream media.

In addition, Dr. Hemphill is one of the Michigan Chronicle Honors 40 Under 40 African American Leaders who exhibited great vision, strong leadership, a love for community, outstanding entrepreneurship, a spirit of philanthropy, and a passion to empower others.

With his first book, *Wrongfully Convicted,* Dr. D hopes to inspire change through the empowerment of God amid the struggles of 21st century living.

CPSIA information can be obtained
at www.ICGtesting.com
Printed in the USA
FFOW03n0617120418
46234232-47618FF